The Wine-Lovers Holidays Cookbook

Menus, Recipes & Wine Selections
For Holiday Entertaining

by

Virginia and Robert Hoffman

The Hoffman Press
Santa Rosa, California

Quantity discounts of this and other Hoffman Press books are available.
Ph: (707) 538-5527   Fax: (707) 538-7371
E-mail: Hoffpress@worldnet.att.net

Visit our web site at <Foodandwinecookbooks.com> to see our other books.

Contents

*I*ntroduction

Each recipe indicates the number of servings. If you are having a smaller or larger number of guests, just change the amounts of the ingredients.

These menus and the recipes are suggestions. Please feel free to move recipes from one menu to another. After all, it is your menu!

We've designed many of these recipes so they may be prepared a day or two before the holiday meal. We have done this so you can enjoy entertaining without staying in the kitchen until the very last minute.

We have suggested wines to accompany these special meals. American wines were selected throughout this book for several reasons: First, because there are great wines produced in America; Second, they are available throughout the United States in wine shops, supermarkets, and from wine clubs, within affordable price ranges; Third, they are based upon our own preferences and those of others in the field of pairing wine with food.

A note about our wine suggestions and what you may prefer. If you like a wine other than the ones we suggest...serve it. Much of the pairing of food with wine is personal, and you and your guests should enjoy the wine of your choice.

We enjoyed writing this cookbook. We hope that you have as much pleasure in using this book as we did in writing it.

Virginia and Robert Hoffman

Wines: "Made in America"

We've compiled this list of varietal wines that are made in America—wines that are made from specific grapes of the same name—as the basis for your selection of wines to accompany foods...or simply to enjoy by the glass. There are many wines that are made from blending two or more varieties, but these are often labeled with the vintner's own brand name. This makes it quite difficult to recommend one wine by brand name over another. That is why we are identifying only varietal wines in this section and in our suggestions for wines to accompany the recipes in this book.

These are wines you should know about. You will enjoy many of them. Some are quite new in America. Others have been, and are, in limited production. All have distinctive attributes that make them special.

There are several excellent sources for these wines. First is visiting the wineries and tasting them there, talking to the people who make the wine. Second are the wine clubs, which are a wonderful resource for wine-lovers. They will not only ship directly to your door, but will introduce you to wineries, varieties and vintages that are often hard to find. Another excellent source is the wine merchant, who can help you find the exact wine that fits your needs.

The Red Wines...

Barbera is a rich, fruity wine with a dark red color. Still quite new in America, it is rapidly overtaking Chianti, from Italy, a favorite wine for many years.

Cabernet Franc was originally used in France in blending Cabernet Sauvignon varieties. When it first came to America it was used for the same purpose, but it has now developed its own following and is being marketed as Cabernet Franc. Very similar to Cabernet Sauvignon, it is a little less intense in flavor, and well suited to accompany many foods.

Cabernet Sauvignon is the classic red wine of France that has become the most popular of all red wines made in America today. Its rich, full flavor and brilliant red color are the perfect accompaniments to many dishes.

Carigniane is a rich, well-bodied table wine that is just now being produced in America. A little heavier than a Barbera, it is a hearty wine to serve with hearty food. Because of its richness, it is ideal, too, for making wine drinks such as coolers.

Gamay (also known as **Gamay Beaujolais**) is a light wine, ideal to accompany salads and light summer meals. It has a nice light fresh fruitiness that is in contrast to many red wines.

Grenache is the lightest in color of the red wines, with a wonderful fruity flavor, and is a nice change from the more full-bodied red wines. This is the second most planted acreage of all varieties, thanks to its ability to withstand heat and require minimal water.

Merlot has become one of America's favorite wines! Similar to Cabernet Sauvignon, but with a slightly mellower taste, it has the ability to accompany a wide variety of foods perfectly. American Merlots have won some international competitions in recent years, thanks to its luscious deep flavors.

Nebbiolo wine is now being produced in America, still in limited quantities. It has an Italian heritage of being one of the great red wines. An alternative to Barbera, it has a delightful tangy taste.

Petit Syrah (also known as Syrah) is a wine with lots of character and peppery overtones. Often used in blending, it adds body to the red wines to which it is added.

Pinot Noir, like Cabernet Sauvignon, is a classic red wine that is becoming increasingly popular in America. Rich and spicy, it adds great dimension to the meal with which it is served. Unlike Cabernet Sauvignon, which adapts readily to new climates and soil conditions, Pinot Noir grapes are more difficult to grow, probably the reason that the wine is a bit more expensive than other red wines.

Sangiovese has come into its own in America, thanks to its rich strawberry/cherry/herbs overtones. Still being produced in America in limited quantities, it is growing in popularity as it becomes more widely available.

Zinfandel is available in a wide range of wines, which include a light Blush, a White Zinfandel, and a dark red full-bodied Zinfandel. Growing in popularity, too, is a Late Harvest Zinfandel, which is a sweet dessert wine, thanks to its increased sugar by the grapes being left on the vine for a long time. A note of warning: Don't hold on to this wine for more than five to six years. It does not store well for long periods of time.

The White Wines...

Champagne (Sparkling Wine) is, easily, the best-selling white wine in America. Originally it was the beverage for New Year's Eve, job promotions and weddings, but it is now served throughout the year and for lesser celebrations. There are many variations within the name. There are dry, medium dry, sweet, blush, made from red grapes, made from white grapes, made in the traditional manner, and made in the charmant or tank process. Tasting is strongly recommended prior to any major purchases.

Chardonnay is the wine of choice for most people who like white wine, and their choice is justified, as there are wide ranges in the kinds of Chardonnay that are vinted today. There are dry, very dry, rich and buttery, and flavors of all types in this popular wine. Second only to Champagne in popularity, Chardonnay is the best-selling white wine in America today.

Chenin Blanc ranges from great, inexpensive dry wines to more complex wines with subtle flavors. Usually quite inexpensive, it is available in very dry and sweet versions. An interesting sidelight to this wine is that Easterners prefer the sweet versions, while Westerns prefer the dry ones.

Gewürztraminer, like Zinfandel, has grown in popularity very rapidly in America. This is a very pleasant white wine that can be quite dry or quite sweet. Its clear and pungent flavor, coupled with its crisp and spicy nuances of flavor, is ideal as a wine to accompany many dishes. A Late Harvest Gewürztraminer, like the Late Harvest Zinfandel, is a very sweet wine, ideal for desserts.

Moscato Canelli/Muscat Canelli or Muscat, is quite new in America. Imported under all three names from Italy for many years, it is now made in the United States. Like many other wines, it ranges from very dry to very sweet.

Pinot Blanc grapes produce a dry, fruity wine that is also used in the making of Sparkling Wine. Similar to Chardonnay, it has slightly less flavor and depth but is the perfect wine to serve with many dishes.

Pinot Gris is sometimes labeled **Pinot Grigio** or as **Tokay**. The principal wine of Hungary, it has recently been vinted in America. It is a full-bodied, somewhat heavy wine, with a spicy overtone. One reviewer has called it "Salmon's best friend."

Riesling, also known as Johannisberg Reisling, has been a classic in Europe for centuries. It has a wide range of flavors and is becoming more and more popular each year. It is now being produced in several states, with most of the grape acreage in California and Washington. It is becoming the wine of choice for many Easterners.

Sauvignon Blanc, at one time, was the most popular white wine made. Today, it is outdistanced by Chardonnay. It is, however, a great wine because it is quite dry and goes so well with many foods. A version of Sauvignon Blanc that is marketed under the name Fumé Blanc is supposedly a bit drier than Sauvignon Blanc, but often it is simply Sauvignon Blanc with a different name.

Viognier has become one of the most sought-after grapes in recent years. Recently introduced to America, it is grown principally in California. While acreage is still relatively small, new plantings should produce a more abundant supply in a few years.

The
Menus,
Recipes
and
Wine Selections

Traditional Thanksgiving Dinner
For Eight

Oysters on the Half Shell
Creamed Corn Soup
Celery - Radishes - Olives
Roast Turkey with Chestnut Stuffing
Giblet Gravy
Cranberry Sauce - Spiced Apples
Mashed Potatoes - Brussels Sprouts
Onions in Cream
Pumpkin Pie - Mincemeat Pie
with Vanilla Ice Cream
Assorted Nuts - Fruit - Chocolate Mints Coffee

The Wines

The ultimate wine to accompany oysters is Champagne (Sparkling Wine). Nothing is comparable. But, if you prefer something else, a dry Chardonnay or Chablis will do, in a white wine. If you prefer a red wine, a Pinot Noir is a fitting companion, too.

For the roast turkey, the ideal choice, in white wine, is Chardonnay—preferably a dry one. Equally satisfactory in a red wine would be a Merlot.

If you're serving pumpkin pie, return to the Champagne (Sparkling Wine) or the Chardonnay or Chablis. If you're serving the mincemeat pie, a Riesling is suggested. Serving both? Champagne is the happy compromise.

If you want to serve just one wine for the entire meal, a dry Chardonnay or a Merlot will be satisfactory.

After dinner, with the nuts, fruit, mints and coffee, a nice Cognac or Brandy—something with at least a few years of aging—will round off the evening.

Oysters on the Half Shell

4 to 8 small oysters or
24 large oysters, halved

Hot sauce (recipe below)
8 lemon wedges

Have the store halve the oysters, and pack them with ice for the trip home. Keep very cold until ready to serve.

On a bed of rock salt, serve on the oyster shells with lemon wedges and hot sauce. (The salt serves to keep the oysters from tipping.)

Bottled oysters can be used instead of fresh oysters. Serve them in small glass bowls embedded in ice, with lemon wedges and hot sauce on the side.

OYSTER HOT SAUCE
1/2 cup catsup
2 tablespoons chili sauce
2 tablespoons Worcester-
    shire sauce

2 tablespoons prepared
    horseradish
1/4 teaspoon salt

Combine all ingredients. Serve at room temperature.

Creamed Corn Soup

3 tablespoons butter	2 cups milk
1 medium onion, thinly sliced	1 tablespoon flour
	1/2 bay leaf
1/2 cup green pepper, finely diced	1 teaspoon salt
	1/4 teaspoon pepper
2 potatoes, thinly sliced	1 can (19 ounces) of
2 cups boiling water	cream-style corn

Heat butter in saucepan, add onion and green pepper and cook gently over medium-low heat for 3 minutes, stirring frequently. Add potatoes and boiling water; bring to a boil. Lower heat, cover and boil for 15 minutes until potatoes are tender.

Mix 1/3 cup of the milk with the flour, stirring until smooth. Add to boiling mixture. Add the rest of milk, bay leaf, salt, pepper, and corn.

Simmer for 15 minutes, stirring frequently. Remove bay leaf. Place the soup in a blender and whip for a minute or two until creamy. Remove. Heat again or serve cold. May be made a day or two ahead.

Chestnut Stuffing

2 pounds chestnuts
2 cups butter
2 cups onions, finely
    minced
2 cups celery, finely minced
10 cups dry bread crumbs

2 teaspoons salt
1 teaspoon dried thyme
1 teaspoon dried marjoram
1 teaspoon dried savory
1 teaspoon dried rosemary

With a sharp paring knife cut a cross on the flat side of each chestnut. Simmer for 5 minutes; remove from water. While hot, remove the shells and inner brown skins. Boil for 20 to 30 minutes until tender. Drain; chop coarsely.

Melt the butter in saucepan, add onions and celery; cook until limp. Add bread crumbs, salt, and spices. Mix thoroughly. Add chestnuts, mix thoroughly.

After the turkey is stuffed, any extra stuffing can be baked in a covered casserole in the oven with the turkey for the last hour.

Roast Turkey

1 whole turkey, 12 to 14   Salt and pepper
   pounds

Preheat oven to 350 degrees. Set aside neck and giblets for gravy.

Wash turkey with cold water, dry, and rub salt and pepper into body cavities. Spoon the stuffing (recipe follows) into body cavities. Do not pack tightly. Close skin with skewers or twine and tie drumsticks together.

Place the turkey on a rack in a roasting pan, uncovered, in oven for 20 minutes per pound. Test after three hours for doneness with a fork to see if juices run clear or with a thermometer for an internal temperature of 175 to 180 degrees. If the turkey gets too dark, place an aluminum foil "tent" over the breast.

Remove from oven, place on platter and allow the turkey to stand for 20 minutes before carving.

Giblet Gravy

Neck and giblets of turkey
4 cups boiling water
2 cups white wine
1 teaspoon salt
4 whole peppercorns
1 sprig parsley

1 medium onion
2 whole cloves
1 carrot
5 tablespoons flour
Salt and pepper

Cover neck and giblets in a saucepan with the 4 cups of boiling water and all ingredients except the flour. Boil for 1 minute. Skim residue, cover and lower heat to simmer contents for 1 hour. Strain the broth to remove the spices, onion and carrot.

Remove meat from neck, and mince giblets and neck meat. Reserve.

Pour off all but 6 tablespoons of the fat from the drippings in the turkey pan. Place roasting pan over low heat and stir in the flour. Cook until thickened and bubbling. Add the broth, stirring. Add chopped neck meat and giblets just before serving. Salt and pepper to taste.

Cranberry Sauce

2 pounds fresh
  cranberries
2 cups water

2 cups brown sugar
1 cup chopped walnuts
1 cup raisins

Cook the cranberries and brown sugar in the water until the cranberries pop open. Reduce to simmer, and add the walnuts and raisins. Simmer for 10 to 15 minutes; refrigerate. May be made up to a week in advance.

Spiced Apples

2 pounds tart cooking
  apples
2 cups sugar

1 pint wine vinegar
1 stick cinnamon
1/2 teaspoon whole cloves

Pare, core, and slice apples horizontally, 1/2 inch thick, cut into quarters. Place all ingredients in a saucepan, bring to a boil and cook for 5 minutes. Reduce to a simmer; cook until tender. Apples remain in syrup until ready to serve. May be made up to a week ahead.

Mashed Potatoes

6 medium potatoes (2
  pounds)
2 tablespoons butter

1/4 cup warm milk
1/4 teaspoon salt
1/4 teaspoon pepper

Peel and quarter potatoes, removing any eyes, dark areas, or other blemishes. Boil for 20 to 25 minutes until tender; drain. Mash with mixer at low speed or with a potato masher until lumps are completely gone. Add the butter and warm milk as you mash and finish with salt and pepper.

Brussels Sprouts

1-1/2 pounds fresh
Brussels sprouts
1 medium yellow onion,
  peeled and sliced

1/4 cup balsamic vinegar
2 tablespoons butter
Salt and pepper

Cut off the stems and remove any limp leaves from the Brussels sprouts. Blanch them in boiling water for 5 minutes. Drain and rinse with cold water to stop the cooking process.

Heat a large frying pan and sauté the onions until translucent. Add the Brussels sprouts. Sauté for a few minutes until they are cooked, but still firm. Add the vinegar and toss to ensure all sprouts are thoroughly coated. Add butter and salt and pepper to taste.

Onions in Cream

3 pounds pearl or very
 small yellow onions
2 cups chicken broth
2 tablespoons butter
6 tablespoons flour
1/3 cup dry sherry

1 cup half-and-half
1/4 teaspoon ground
 nutmeg
1 tablespoon fresh parsley,
 chopped

Preheat oven to 375 degrees.

Trim and peel onions, placing them in a saucepan. Add the chicken broth and bring to a boil. Cover and simmer for 10 minutes, or until just tender. Strain, remove onions, and put them aside. Continue simmering stock.

Melt the butter in a small frying pan, and add flour. Cook together for a few minutes, but do not allow them to get brown. Add this to the stock, and stir until thickened and smooth. Stir in the sherry and half-and-half. Simmer for 2 minutes more. Add nutmeg and parsley.

Combine the onions with the sauce in a casserole and bake for 40 to 45 minutes at 375 degrees, until it is bubbling. Brown, if you wish, under the broiler.

Pumpkin Pie

Pastry for single crust pie (see note)
1 can (16 ounces) pumpkin
3/4 cup sugar
1 teaspoon ground cinnamon
1/2 teaspoon ground ginger
1/2 teaspoon ground nutmeg
1/2 teaspoon salt
3 eggs
2/3 cup (15-ounce can) evaporated milk
1/2 cup milk

Preheat oven to 375 degrees.

In a large bowl, combine pumpkin, sugar, all spices, salt, and the eggs. Lightly beat eggs into the mixture with fork. Add the milk and evaporated milk; mix thoroughly.

Line a 9-inch pie plate with the pastry shell, trim, and fill with pumpkin mixture. Cover rim of pie with foil. Bake for 25 minutes, remove foil and return to oven for 25 minutes more or until knife inserted in center comes out clean. Cool.

Cover and chill to serve. Whipped cream or ice cream are optional.

Note: Purchase a refrigerated pie shell, or use your favorite pie pastry recipe.

Mincemeat Pie

Pastry for a double crust
   pie (see note)
1/2 cup raisins
1/4 cup brandy
2 cups mincemeat

1/2 cup orange marmalade
2 tablespoons flour
1 tablespoon lemon juice
1/4 teaspoon ground
   nutmeg

Preheat oven to 425 degrees.

Soak the raisins in the brandy for at least an hour. Combine all ingredients except pastry shell; mix thoroughly. Line a 9-inch pie plate with one pastry shell, fill, and place second pastry shell over all. Crimp top shell over bottom and trim excess. Perforate top shell, and if desired, sprinkle lightly with milk and sugar, to achieve more browning.

Bake for 45 to 50 minutes. Serve warm. May be topped with ice cream.

Note: Purchase refrigerated pie shells, or use your favorite pie pastry recipe.

A New England Thanksgiving Dinner
For Eight

Carrot Bisque
Roast Turkey with Molasses Glaze
Giblet Gravy - Cornbread-Sage Dressing
Mashed Parsnip Potatoes
Red Pepper Succotash
Cranberry Relish with Pears & Apples
Classic New England Cider Pie
Spiced Walnuts
Coffee - Tea

The Wines

It is probable that a red wine was served...if any wine was served at all...at the first Thanksgiving dinner hosted by the Pilgrims, as that was the wine of choice in England. We are more fortunate today in the wines available to us.

We suggest that, in white wines, a dry Chardonnay will go very well with this menu. A Riesling that is not too flowery or sweet would be a good second choice. A third is Viognier, relatively new in America, that you and your guests will enjoy.

In red wines, our first choice is a rich Pinot Noir, or a Cabernet Sauvignon, both with a few years of vintage. Another very satisfactory wine with this menu would be a good Zinfandel. And if that is not enough of a choice, a Grenache or a Cabernet Franc would be very satisfactory.

Carrot Bisque

1/4 cup plus 2 tablespoons butter

2 pounds carrots, peeled and sliced thin

2 large onions, chopped

1 tablespoon peeled, minced fresh ginger

2 teaspoons grated orange peel

1/2 teaspoon ground coriander

5 cups chicken broth

1 cup half-and-half

1/2 cup fresh parsley, minced

Salt and pepper

Melt butter in heavy large saucepan over medium heat. Add carrots and onions. Cover saucepan and cook until vegetables begin to soften, stirring occasionally, about 15 minutes. Mix in ginger, orange peel, and coriander. Add 2 cups of the broth.

Reduce heat to medium low. Cover pan and simmer soup until carrots are very tender, about 30 minutes.

Purée soup in batches in blender. Add remaining 3 cups broth and the half-and-half to soup. Season with salt and pepper This soup can be prepared ahead and re-heated later.

Heat over medium heat until warm. Serve with a sprinkle of parsley.

Cornbread-Sage Dressing

5 cups coarse cornbread
  crumbs or purchased mix
7 tablespoons butter
3 large celery stalks,
  chopped
2 medium onions, chopped
3 tablespoons fresh sage,
  chopped, or 1 tablespoon
  dried, crumbled sage

3/4 teaspoon salt
1/2 teaspoon pepper
4 cups 1/2-inch cubes
  white bread
3/4 cup chicken stock or
  canned low-salt broth
1 egg, beaten to blend

Preheat oven to 350 degrees. Butter one large or two medium casserole dishes.

If you are making cornbread crumbs, crumble cornbread coarsely onto a large cookie sheet. Let stand uncovered at room temperature overnight to dry.

Melt butter in a heavy large skillet over medium heat. Add celery and onions to cook until tender, stirring frequently, about 12 minutes. Transfer mixture to large bowl. Mix in sage, salt, and pepper. (This stage can be prepared 1 day ahead. Cover and refrigerate.) Add cornbread crumbs or packaged mix, and bread cubes to vegetables. Combine the stock and egg in a small bowl. Stir into dressing.

Note: Bake dressing alongside the turkey for final 30 minutes and while turkey stands at room temperature.

Roast Turkey with Molasses Glaze

1 whole turkey 15 pounds
Salt and pepper
Poultry seasoning
1 onion, peeled
3 tablespoons butter, melted
2 cups plus 2 tablespoons chicken stock

1 tablespoon dark molasses
1 teaspoon red wine vinegar
Fresh sage sprigs (optional)

Preheat oven to 350 degrees. Rinse turkey inside and out. Set aside neck and giblets. Dry thoroughly. Discard any fat in neck or main cavity. Season neck cavity with salt and pepper. Fold neck skin over and secure to body with skewer. Season main body cavity with salt, pepper and poultry seasoning. Place onion in cavity. Sew or skewer main cavity closed. Tuck wings under turkey body. Tie legs together.

Place turkey, breast side up, on rack in large roasting pan. Brush 2 tablespoons of the melted butter over turkey. Pour 1/2 cup stock or broth into pan.

Roast turkey 2-1/2 hours, basting with pan juices, and adding 1/2 cup chicken stock to pan about every 45 minutes. Combine remaining 1 tablespoon melted butter with molasses and vinegar. Brush glaze over turkey.

Roast turkey about 30 minutes longer, until meat thermometer inserted into thickest part of thigh registers 175 degrees. Transfer turkey to platter and tent with foil. Let stand 20 to 30 minutes before carving.

Giblet Gravy

7 tablespoons flour
5 cups giblet broth (recipe
  follows) or canned low-
  salt chicken broth

1/3 cup dry sherry
Salt and pepper

Pour turkey pan juices from roasting pan into a bowl. Degrease juices in the bowl, reserving 6 tablespoons fat. Pour reserved fat back into the pan. Place pan over medium heat. Add the flour to the roasting pan and whisk until beginning to brown, about 3 minutes. Gradually whisk in giblet broth, de-greased pan juices, and sherry. Simmer until gravy thickens, whisking and scraping bottom of pan, about 10 minutes. Mix in giblets and neck meat from giblet broth. Season with salt and pepper. Transfer gravy to sauceboat or serving dish.

Giblet Broth for Gravy

6 cups low-salt chicken
  broth
Neck and giblets reserved
  from turkey
1 small onion, halved

2 celery stalks with tops,
  coarsely chopped
1/4 teaspoon dried,
  crumbled sage
Pinch of pepper

Combine all ingredients except turkey liver in a heavy large saucepan and bring to boil. Reduce heat, cover partially and simmer 1 1/2 hours. Rinse liver and add to broth.

Simmer until liver is cooked through, about 10 minutes. Remove giblets and reserve. Strain broth, discarding vegetables. Carefully remove neck meat from bones. Finely chop giblets and neck meat and reserve for gravy. Cover and chill broth and chopped meats separately until ready to use.

Mashed Parsnip Potatoes

4 pounds russet potatoes,
  peeled
1-1/2 pounds parsnips,
  peeled

1/2 cup (1 stick) butter
2 green onions, chopped
1-1/2 cups milk
Parsley for garnish

Cut the potatoes and parsnips into 1 1/2-inch pieces. Add them to large pot of salted water and boil until very tender, about 20 minutes. Drain well. While the potatoes drain, melt butter in same pot over low heat. Add onions and sauté 1 minute. Add milk and bring just to simmer. Add potatoes and parsnips to pot; mash until smooth. Season with salt and pepper.

This recipe can be prepared ahead to this point. Let stand at room temperature.

Heat mashed potato mixture over low heat until hot, stirring frequently. Transfer to bowl, garnish with chopped parsley and serve.

Red Pepper Succotash

6 cups frozen lima beans
6 cups frozen corn kernels
1-1/2 cups, red bell
   pepper, finely chopped
   (about 1 1/2 peppers)
3 tablespoons butter

1 cup plus 2 tablespoons
   cream
1/2 teaspoon sugar
Salt and pepper
Minced fresh parsley for
   garnish

Cook lima beans for about 6 minutes in a large saucepan of boiling water until almost tender. Add corn and bring to simmer. Add red pepper and cook 2 minutes. Drain well.

Return vegetables to the same saucepan. Add butter and toss to coat. Add cream and cook over medium heat until sauce thickens, stirring occasionally, for about 10 minutes. Add sugar. Season with salt and pepper to taste. Transfer to bowl. Sprinkle with parsley.

Cranberry Relish with Pears and Apples

3 tart apples, such as
    Granny Smith or Pippin,
    peeled, cored and diced
2 ripe pears, peeled, cored
    and diced
2 pounds fresh cranberries
2 cups sugar
1 cup golden raisins

1 cup freshly squeezed
    orange juice
2 tablespoons grated
    orange rind
2 teaspoons ground
    cinnamon
1/4 teaspoon ground
    nutmeg
1/2 cup brandy

Mix together all the ingredients except the brandy in a saucepan. Bring to a boil, reduce the heat and simmer, uncovered, for 45 minutes, until thick. Stir in the brandy, let cool to room temperature, and refrigerate, covered, until serving time.

Classic New England Cider Pie

Pastry for a double crust pie (see note)

2-1/2 cups apple cider

2-1/2 pounds tart apples (about 6) peeled, cored and sliced

1 pound Golden Delicious apples (about 2) peeled, cored and sliced

1 cup sugar

1/4 cup all-purpose flour

1/2 teaspoon ground cinnamon

1/4 teaspoon ground mace

1/4 teaspoon salt

4 teaspoons fresh lemon juice

3 tablespoons butter, cut into small pieces

Let pie crusts soften at room temperature before using.

Boil cider for about 25 minutes in heavy small saucepan until reduced to 2/3 cup. Cool.

Position rack in lowest third of oven and preheat to 425 degrees. Combine all apples, sugar, flour, cinnamon, mace, and salt in a large bowl. Add reduced cider and lemon juice and toss well.

Roll out 1 pie crust disk on a lightly floured surface to a 14-inch round. Transfer to 10-inch pie plate. Gently press into place. Trim edges of crust, leaving 1/2-inch overhang. Spoon apples into crust-lined pan, mounding in center. Dot with butter. Roll out second disk on the lightly floured surface to a 13-inch round and gently place over pie. Trim edges, leaving 3/4 inch overhang. Fold overhang of top crust under edge of bottom crust. Pinch together to seal.

Crimp edges to make decorative border. Cut slashes in top crust to allow steam to escape.

Bake pie 25 minutes, then reduce oven temperature to 350 degrees. Continue baking until filling bubbles, about 50 minutes longer. Cover edges with foil if browning too quickly. Cool. Serve pie warm or at room temperature.

Note: Purchase refrigerated pie shells, or use your favorite pie pastry recipe.

Spiced Walnuts

3 cups walnuts
2 tablespoons vegetable
   oil
1 teaspoon ground cumin

1/4 teaspoon cayenne
   pepper
2 tablespoons sugar
1 teaspoon salt

Preheat oven to 300 degrees. Place the nuts in a bowl.

Pour the oil into a small, heavy saucepan and place over medium-low heat until warm. Add the cumin and cayenne and stir until the mixture is aromatic, about 15 seconds. Pour the flavored oil over the nuts. Add the sugar and salt and stir to coat evenly. Transfer the nuts to a baking pan.

Bake, stirring occasionally, until the nuts are toasted, about 20 minutes. These are best served hot.

May be stored in an airtight container for up to 2 weeks. Reheat for about 5 minutes before serving.

Southern Thanksgiving Dinner
For Eight

Watercress Soup
Roast Turkey with Oyster Stuffing
Country Green Beans with Ham and Onions
Sweet Potato Apricot Bake
Corn Pudding - Cranberry-Ginger Chutney
Cheddar Cheese Biscuits
Pumpkin Pie
Coffee - Tea

The Wines

Sauvignon Blanc is our first choice to serve with this menu, with Chardonnay as an acceptable second choice. If you prefer a red wine, a Zinfandel (preferably from older, more mature vines) is recommended. A second, and very good choice, too, would be a Pinot Noir.

If you plan on serving a white and a red wine, the Chardonnay and the Pinot Noir is suggested.

The Chardonnay is particularly good with the pumpkin pie.

Watercress Soup

1/2 pound butter or
  margarine
2 medium onions, peeled
  and chopped
4 bunches watercress
1/2 cup flour

4 cups chicken broth,
  low-salt
2 cups milk
Salt and freshly ground
  pepper

Melt butter in saucepan, add onion and cook gently for 10 minutes until soft. Set aside.

Wash and trim the watercress, removing most of the stems, but leaving a few. Chop coarsely. Add the watercress to the onions, cover pan, and cook gently for 4 minutes.

Add flour, cook gently, stirring, for 2 minutes. Remove from heat and gradually add broth and milk. Bring to a boil, then simmer for 4 minutes. Add salt and pepper to taste.

Puree in a blender or food processor. This soup may be prepared a day or two ahead, and gently reheated when ready to serve.

Country Green Beans
with Ham and Onions

2 pounds fresh green
  beans, trimmed
1/2 pound 1/4-inch-thick
  sliced country ham, cut
  into 2-inch strips
1 cup chopped onion

1/3 cup cider vinegar
1 tablespoon sugar
1/2 teaspoon ground black
pepper
1 teaspoon salt

Add salt, then green beans to large pot of boiling water. Cook for about 6 minutes until beans are just tender. Drain beans and rinse under cold water. Drain again and pat dry. Reserve.

Cook ham in large skillet over medium heat until brown and crisp. Remove from skillet to paper towels to drain. Pour off all but 1 tablespoon drippings. Add the onion to the skillet; sauté for 3 to 5 minutes or until tender.

Add ham to the skillet along with the vinegar, sugar, and pepper. Cook, stirring, until sugar is dissolved and mixture is hot and bubbly. Add cooked beans; toss to coat and heat through. Serve immediately.

Roast Turkey with Oyster Stuffing

1 loaf white bread (1
   pound)
2 cups finely chopped
   celery (7 to 8 stalks)
2 cups finely chopped
   onion (2 to 3 medium
   onions)
3/4 cup butter or
   margarine (1-1/2 sticks)
1/2 cup milk

24 ounces (3 containers)
   fresh, frozen or canned
   small oysters, drained
1 teaspoon lemon juice
1/4 teaspoon ground
   nutmeg
3/4 teaspoon poultry
   seasoning
Salt and pepper
1 whole turkey 12 to 14
   pounds

Dry bread slices overnight in open air or on a rack in 250 degree oven 1 to 1-1/4 hours.

In skillet, sauté celery and onion in butter until tender. Warm milk over low heat in small saucepan. Tear bread into 1/2-inch pieces, making about 11 cups; place in large mixing bowl. Sprinkle warm milk over bread, tossing lightly. Add onion and celery with butter mixture and oysters to bread; toss to mix well. Sprinkle with lemon juice, nutmeg, poultry seasoning, 1/4 teaspoon salt and 1/4 teaspoon pepper; mix thoroughly.

Preheat oven to 325 degrees. Rinse turkey; pat dry. Rub salt and pepper into neck and body cavities. Lightly spoon dressing into neck cavity; close with skewer. Fill body cavity. Secure drumsticks with a string. Roast uncovered on roasting rack for 20 to 22 minutes per pound or to internal temperature of 170 to 180 degrees. Let turkey stand at least 20 minutes before carving.

Sweet Potato Apricot Bake

2-1/4 pounds (about 6)
  medium yams, cooked,
  drained and pared
1/4 cup plus 2 tablespoons
  packed light brown sugar
1 tablespoon all-purpose
  flour
1/2 teaspoon ground
  cinnamon
1/8 teaspoon salt

1-1/2 cups orange juice
2 tablespoons butter
1 tablespoon orange
  liqueur (optional)
2 to 3 teaspoons grated
  orange rind
1 cup dried apricots,
  halved or quartered
1/4 cup golden raisins
1 cup pecans, chopped

Preheat oven to 350 degrees.

Cut the yams or sweet potatoes in half lengthwise; place in a single layer in a 2-quart shallow baking dish.

Combine 1/4 cup of the brown sugar, flour, cinnamon, and salt in a medium saucepan. Mix well. gradually stir in the orange juice until the mixture is well blended and smooth. Bring the mixture to boiling over medium heat; cook, stirring constantly for 1 minute.

Remove from heat; stir in the butter until melted. Add the orange liqueur, if using, the orange rind, apricots, and raisins. Pour the mixture over the potatoes in the baking dish. Sprinkle with the pecans and the remaining 2 table-spoons brown sugar.

Bake for 30 minutes or until hot and bubbly.

Corn Pudding

3 tablespoons butter
1-1/2 medium onions,
 chopped
1/4 cup flour
3 eggs

4 cups fresh corn kernels,
 or frozen corn kernels,
 thawed
1-1/2 cups milk
1-1/4 teaspoons salt
Pepper

Position rack in center of oven and preheat to 350 degrees. Butter two 6-cup casserole dishes. Set aside. Melt butter in heavy large skillet over medium heat. Add onions and sauté until very soft, about 12 minutes. Mix in flour and stir 4 minutes. Transfer to bowl and cool to lukewarm.

Add eggs to onion mixture and whisk to blend. Mix in corn, milk, and salt. Season with pepper. Divide batter evenly between prepared dishes. Bake puddings until knife inserted into center of each comes out clean, about 1 hour. Spoon onto plates.

Cranberry-Ginger Chutney

1-1/4 cups fresh
 cranberries
16 dried apricots,
 quartered
3/4 cup packed golden
 brown sugar
1/4 cup dried currants

2 tablespoons peeled,
 minced fresh ginger
2 tablespoons cranberry
 juice cocktail
3/4 teaspoon ground
 cinnamon
1/4 teaspoon cayenne pepper

Combine all ingredients in heavy medium saucepan. Cook over medium heat, stirring to dissolve sugar. Increase heat to high and boil 3 minutes. Transfer to bowl. Cool. This chutney may be prepared up to 1 week ahead. Refrigerate in airtight container.

Cheddar Cheese Biscuits

1-1/4 cups all-purpose flour
1-1/2 teaspoons baking
powder
1/2 teaspoon salt
2 tablespoons solid
vegetable shortening

3 tablespoons shredded
cheddar cheese
1/2 cup buttermilk
1/4 cup chopped green
onions
Butter

Preheat oven to 425 degrees. Lightly butter one large cookie sheet.

Combine flour, baking powder, and salt in bowl. Add shortening and cut in until mixture resembles coarse meal. Stir in cheese. Add buttermilk and onions, and mix well. Turn out dough onto lightly floured surface and roll out to thickness of 1/4 inch.

Cut out biscuits using a 1-1/4-inch round biscuit cutter. Transfer biscuits to prepared cookie sheet.

Bake until puffed and light golden, about 15 minutes. Serve warm. The biscuits can be prepared ahead and re-heated before serving.

Pumpkin Pie

Pastry for a single crust
pie (see note)
2 eggs, slightly beaten
3/4 cup sugar
1-1/2 teaspoons ground
cinnamon
1/2 teaspoon ground
nutmeg
1/2 teaspoon ground
ginger
1/4 teaspoon ground
allspice
1/4 teaspoon ground
cloves
1/2 teaspoon salt
1 can (1 pound) pumpkin
3 tablespoons molasses
2 cans (6 ounces each)
evaporated milk
1 egg white, unbeaten
1/4 cup pecans, finely
chopped
8 whole pecan halves
Whipped cream (optional)

Preheat oven to 400 degrees.

To make the filling, combine eggs, sugar, spices, salt, pumpkin, molasses, and evaporated milk in a large bowl. Combine with a wooden spoon until mixture is smooth.

Lightly brush pie shell with egg white. Sprinkle chopped pecans in bottom of pie shell. Fill with pumpkin mixture. Gently arrange pecan halves on filling around edge of pie.

Bake 55 to 60 minutes or until tip of sharp knife inserted in center comes out clean. Let cool on wire rack. Serve garnished with whipped cream, if using.

Note: Purchase a refrigerated pie shell, or use your favorite pie pastry recipe.

A New England Christmas Dinner For Eight

Oysters on the Half Shell
Pumpkin Soup
Roast Beef with Glazed Onions and Gravy
Celeried Mashed Potatoes
Broccoli with Hazelnuts
Cranberry Horseradish Relish
Rolls
Chocolate Butterscotch Pie
Coffee - Tea

The Wines

If you are serving several wines with this dinner, we suggest a dry Champagne (Sparkling Wine) with the oysters and pumpkin soup, and then going to a good...really good Cabernet Sauvignon. Roast Beef needs a good classic red wine, and a Cabernet Sauvignon with a few years (at least) of aging is the ideal wine.

Nearly as good...and in some minds better...is a good Merlot. With slightly less body, it is a happy solution for those who want a less dominating wine, but still want a hearty red.

In white wines we suggest a good Chardonnay as a first choice with a dry Sauvignon Blanc or Fumé Blanc as a second choice.

If you would like to add another touch of elegance to this menu, serve a Brandy with the dessert and for after-dinner conversation.

Oysters on the Half Shell

4 to 6 small oysters per
  person

Hot sauce (recipe below)
8 lemon wedges

Have the store pack the oysters with ice for the trip home. Keep very cold until ready to serve. Serve on a bed of rock salt in the shells with lemon wedges and hot sauce. (The salt serves to keep the oysters from tipping.) Bottled oysters may be used instead of fresh oysters. Serve them in small glass bowls embedded in ice, with lemon wedges and hot sauce on the side.

OYSTER HOT SAUCE

1/2 cup catsup
2 tablespoons chili sauce
2 tablespoons Worcester-
  shire sauce

2 tablespoons prepared
  horseradish
1/4 teaspoon salt

Combine all ingredients. Serve at room temperature.

Pumpkin Soup

1 tablespoon oil
2 small onions, minced
3 cups chicken broth
1 can (16 ounces)
  prepared pumpkin
1/4 teaspoon ginger curry
  seasoning

1/4 teaspoon ground nutmeg
1 cup evaporated milk
1/4 teaspoon cayenne pepper
1/4 teaspoon ground allspice
1/4 teaspoon ground
  cinnamon
Chopped chives

Heat a 3- or 4-quart saucepan on medium heat. When pan is hot, add oil and heat for an additional minute. Add onions and sauté for about 4 to 5 minutes until translucent. Add chicken broth and pumpkin. Mix thoroughly. Reduce heat and simmer for 15 minutes. Add seasonings and evaporated milk; simmer for an additional 5 minutes. Garnish with chopped chives.

Roast Beef with
Glazed Onions and Gravy

2 large onions, sliced thin
1 can (14 to 16 ounces)
  crushed tomatoes
1-1/2 tablespoons
  vegetable oil
Salt and pepper
4-pound boneless rib roast
  (at room temperature)

2 tablespoons all-purpose
  flour
2 cups beef broth
1/2 cup sweet vermouth
1/2 cup water
Fresh rosemary sprigs for
  garnish

Preheat oven to 500 degrees. In a roasting pan, thoroughly combine the onions, tomatoes, oil, and salt and pepper to taste. Roast the mixture in the middle of a the oven for 10 minutes. Stir the mixture, put the beef, seasoned with salt and pepper, on top of it, and roast the beef and the onion mixture in the oven for 15 minutes. Reduce the temperature to 350 degrees and roast the beef for 12 minutes more per pound, or until a meat thermometer registers 135 degrees, for medium-rare meat.

Transfer the beef to a cutting board and let it stand for 30 minutes. To the onion mixture, add the flour and cook over moderate heat, stirring, for 3 minutes. Whisk in the broth, vermouth, and water. Simmer the gravy, whisking and scraping up the brown bits, for 10 to 15 minutes. Let stand; skim any fat from the top. Reheat. Serve in gravy boat. Carve roast beef just before serving. Serve with gravy.

Celeried Mashed Potatoes

3 pounds russet (baking)
potatoes, scrubbed
4 tablespoons unsalted
butter

5 cups chopped celery,
including the leaves
(about 1/2 bunch)
1 clove garlic, pressed
1 cup milk, scalded

Preheat oven to 375 degrees.

Prick the potatoes a few times with a fork and bake them in the middle of the oven for 1 hour.

In a large skillet, melt the butter over moderate heat. In it cook the celery and the garlic, covered, for 10 minutes. Cook the mixture, uncovered, stirring, for 10 minutes more, or until the celery is tender.

Transfer the mixture to a food processor and purée it. Peel the baked potatoes and force them through a ricer into a bowl. (Alternatively, the potatoes may be mashed with a potato masher.) Stir in the celery purée, salt and pepper to taste, and enough of the milk to reach the desired consistency.

Broccoli with Hazelnuts

1 onion, chopped
1 cup toasted and chopped
   hazelnuts
3 tablespoons butter
2 tablespoons water

2 heads fresh broccoli or
   2 packages frozen,
   chopped broccoli.
Salt and freshly ground
   black pepper

Sauté the onion and hazelnuts in the butter until the onion is translucent. Add the water and the broccoli. Cover and cook on low heat until the broccoli is tender. Add a small amount of water during cooking, if necessary, to keep the vegetables from sticking to the pan. Add salt and pepper to taste.

Cranberry Horseradish Relish

4 cups fresh cranberries
1/2 cup sugar

2/3 cup prepared
   horseradish

Sort the cranberries, discarding soft ones. Chop cranberries and put into a medium saucepan with the sugar. Heat over medium heat, stirring constantly until the sugar dissolves and the mixture is fully blended, about 5 minutes. Turn heat to low and simmer for 15 minutes. Set aside to cool. When cranberries are cool, stir in the horseradish and serve.

Chocolate Butterscotch Pie

Prepared pastry for crust
2 ounces unsweetened
  chocolate, chopped
2 cups firmly packed
  golden brown sugar
1/2 cup (1 stick) butter, at
  room temperature
3 large eggs

1/2 cup whipping cream
1 cup chilled whipping
  cream
1 tablespoon confectioners'
  sugar
Grated semi-sweet
  chocolate

Preheat oven to 400 degrees. Line 9-inch glass pie dish with crust. Crimp edges. Butter a large piece of foil. Place foil, buttered-side down, in crust. Bake 10 minutes. Remove foil and bake crust 5 minutes more, piercing crust with fork if bubbles appear. Cool completely.

Reduce oven temperature to 350 degrees. Melt unsweetened chocolate in top of a double boiler over simmering water, stirring until chocolate is smooth. Cool. Using an electric mixer, beat brown sugar and butter in a medium bowl until blended. Add the eggs, one at a time, beating well after each addition. Stir in 1/2 cup cream and melted chocolate.

Pour filling into prepared pie crust. Bake until filling is set, about 45 minutes. Cool pie completely. This stage can be prepared 2 hours ahead.

In a large bowl, beat the 1 cup chilled cream and confectioners' sugar to stiff peaks. Spread cream over pie. Sprinkle with grated chocolate and serve.

Southern Christmas Dinner
For Eight

Lobster Bisque - Cornbread Croutons
Ham with Mustard-Apple Glaze
Apple and Pear Chutney
Potato-Celery Root Purée
Gingered Carrots
Green Beans with Red Bell Pepper
Sweet Potato Biscuits
Pecan Maple Syrup Pie
Cinnamon Chocolate Pie with Whipped Cream
Coffee - Tea

The Wines

A white wine such as a Riesling will go very well with the lobster bisque, followed by a Pinot Noir or a Merlot to accompany the main course.

If you want to compromise on a white wine to serve for the entire meal, a dry Chardonnay, preferably with three to five years barrel aging, would be good. Even better, we suggest that your guests have a choice between the Chardonnay and a Pinot Noir or Merlot. The mustard-apple glaze adds a distinctive flavor to the roast ham, and many prefer a red wine for that reason.

You have two desserts suggested. Either will be good with Champagne (Sparkling Wine). An alternative would be a delightful wine, not too well known, called Eiswin or Icewine.

Lobster Bisque

2 teaspoons minced onion
3 tablespoons butter
3 tablespoons flour
2 tablespoons tomato paste
3 cups hot chicken broth

2 cups minced, cooked
  lobster meat
1 cup milk
2 cups cream
Salt and cayenne pepper

Sauté the onion in the butter until tender. Add the flour and tomato paste. Stir until completely blended. Add broth. Cook until slightly thickened, stirring all the time. Add lobster meat.

Cook over low heat for 10 minutes. Stir in milk and cream. Continue heating mixture. Do not let boil. Season with salt and cayenne pepper to taste before serving. Serve bisque with cornbread croutons (recipe follows).

Cornbread Croutons

1 tablespoon olive oil
2 corn muffins, cut into
  1/3-inch cubes

Salt and pepper

In a skillet (preferably non-stick) heat oil over moderately high heat until hot. Sauté corn muffin cubes until golden brown and crisp. Season croutons with salt and pepper to taste. Croutons may be made one day ahead and kept in a sealed plastic bag. Reheat in oven before serving.

Ham with Mustard-Apple Glaze

1 skinless smoke-cured
  ham, 12 to 14-pounds
Whole cloves for studding

1/2 cup apple jelly
2 tablespoons Dijon
  mustard

Preheat oven to 350 degrees. Score top of ham into diamonds and stud center of each diamond with a clove. Bake ham in a roasting pan in the middle of the oven for 1-1/2 hours.

In a small saucepan heat jelly over moderate heat, stirring constantly until melted and smooth. Remove saucepan from heat and stir in mustard. Spread glaze evenly on top of the baked ham and bake 35 minutes more. Let stand 15 minutes before carving to serve.

Apple and Pear Chutney

1 firm red pear, cored and
  chopped
3 tart apples, cored and
  chopped
1 cup golden raisins
1/4 cup wine vinegar
1/4 cup sugar

1 tablespoon fresh ginger,
  peeled and minced
1 teaspoon mustard seeds
1/4 teaspoon ground
  cinnamon
1/4 teaspoon ground
  nutmeg

In a saucepan combine pear and apples with remaining ingredients and bring to a simmer, stirring gently. Simmer, covered, stirring occasionally, until fruit is tender, 10 to 15 minutes; cool. Chutney may be made ahead and refrigerated. Serve chilled.

Potato-Celery Root Purée

3 large russet potatoes,
   peeled and cut into
   2-inch pieces
1 medium celery root (or
   celeriac), peeled and cut
   into small pieces

1/2 cup cream
1/4 cup butter
2 tablespoons orange
   rind, finely grated
Salt and black pepper

Place the potatoes and celery root in a saucepan with water to cover vegetables. Place over high heat and bring the water to a boil. Reduce to a simmer and cook until tender.

Heat the cream and the butter in a saucepan until the butter is melted. Drain the potatoes and celery root, then mash. Quickly fold in the hot cream mixture and the orange rind. Season with salt and black pepper.

Gingered Carrots

3 pounds carrots, cut into
   3 x 1/2-inch sticks
3 tablespoons brown sugar
3 tablespoons butter

1 tablespoon fresh ginger
   peeled, finely chopped
   fresh ginger
Salt and pepper

Cover carrots with salted water by 2 inches and boil, uncovered, until tender, about 10 minutes. While carrots are cooking, in a small saucepan cook brown sugar, butter, and ginger over moderate heat, stirring, until butter is melted. Drain carrots well and toss them in a bowl with the brown sugar glaze and salt and pepper to taste.

Green Beans with Red Bell Pepper

1 pound green beans,
  trimmed
3 tablespoons butter

1 red bell pepper, cut into
  julienne strips

In a large saucepan of boiling salted water, cook the beans for 3 minutes. Drain and plunge them into a bowl of ice and cold water to stop the cooking. Let the beans cool completely and drain well. The beans may be prepared a day in advance if kept covered and refrigerated.

In a skillet, heat the butter over moderately high heat. Cook the beans and the bell pepper, stirring, for 2 minutes or until the vegetables are crisp-tender.

Sweet Potato Biscuits

1 can (1 pound) sweet
   potatoes, mashed
2-1/4 cups buttermilk
   biscuit mix
1/2 cup firmly packed
   brown sugar

1 teaspoon ground
   cinnamon
1/2 teaspoon ground
   ginger
1/2 teaspoon ground
   nutmeg
3 tablespoons water

Preheat oven to 350 degrees.

Grease a large baking sheet. Put mashed sweet potatoes in a bowl. Stir in buttermilk biscuit mix, sugar, and spices. Add enough water, by tablespoons, to form soft dough.

Turn out the dough onto a lightly floured surface. Pat the dough into 1/2-inch thick round. Cut out the biscuits using a small round biscuit or cookie cutter.

Transfer biscuits to the prepared baking sheet, spacing evenly. Bake until golden brown, about 18 minutes (biscuits will rise only slightly). Transfer biscuits to racks. Serve warm or at room temperature.

Pecan-Maple Syrup Pie

1 9-inch prepared pie crust
3 eggs
1 cup maple syrup
1/4 cup dark corn syrup
1/4 cup sugar

1/4 cup unsalted butter, melted
1 teaspoon vanilla extract
1/4 teaspoon salt
1-1/2 cups pecan halves

Preheat oven to 425 degrees. Roll out the pastry and line a 9-inch pie pan. Set aside.

In a large bowl, beat the eggs until blended. Add the maple syrup, corn syrup, sugar, butter, vanilla and salt. Beat until thoroughly combined. Stir in pecan halves.

Pour the pecan mixture into the pastry-lined pan. Bake for 15 minutes, then reduce the heat to 350 degrees and bake until the filling has puffed and set around the edges, but the center is slightly soft, about 25 minutes longer. Serve warm or at room temperature.

Cinnamon Chocolate Pie

Pastry for a single crust pie

FILLING:

1 cup light corn syrup
1/2 cup sugar
1/4 cup margarine or
  butter, melted
1 teaspoon vanilla extract
1 teaspoon ground
  cinnamon

3 eggs
1 (6-ounce) package
  (1 cup) semi-sweet
  chocolate chips
1-1/2 cups pecan halves

TOPPING:

Whipped cream
1/2 teaspoon ground
  cinnamon

1 teaspoon confectioners'
  sugar

Prepare pie crust for a 9-inch pie. Heat oven to 325 degrees.

In a large bowl, combine corn syrup, sugar, margarine, vanilla, cinnamon, and eggs and beat well. Stir in the chocolate chips and pecans. Spread the mixture evenly in pie crust-lined pan. Bake for 55 to 65 minutes or until deep golden brown and filling is set. Cover edge of pie crust with strip of foil after 15 to 20 minutes of baking to prevent excessive browning. Cool completely.

Garnish pie with whipped cream to which you have added the cinnamon and powdered sugar. Keep pie refrigerated until serving.

A Roast Goose Christmas Dinner
For Eight

Pumpkin Soup
Roast Goose with Port Giblet Gravy
Apple-Sage Dressing
Nutmeg Mashed Potatoes
Glazed Carrots and Parsnips
Spiced Red Cabbage
Fresh Cranberry Relish
Pecan Tarts - Apple and Mince Tart
Coffee - Tea

The Wines

The rich meat of roast goose requires one of two types of wine. In Central Europe, where roast goose is more frequently served than in the United States, white wines such as Riesling and Gewürztraminer are usually served. In the United States, red wines such as Cabernet Sauvignon, Pinot Noir and Merlot, are more popular.

The white wines noted have a semi-sweetness that comple-ments the richness of the goose meat. The red wines noted contrast with this richness. This decision is up to you. We suggest that you serve both to please everyone.

With dessert, and for afterwards, a Late Harvest Zinfandel or a Muscat Canelli will round off this elegant dinner.

Pumpkin Soup

4 tablespoons unsalted
  butter
1/4 cup green onions,
  finely chopped
3 large white potatoes,
  peeled and cut in cubes
4 cups chicken broth

1 can (1 pound 13
  ounces) pumpkin,
  mashed
2 cups heavy cream
1/4 cup sherry
Salt and pepper
Grated nutmeg

In a deep soup pot, melt butter over medium-low heat. Add green onions and cook, stirring until transparent and wilted; do not brown. Add cubed potatoes and 1 cup of the chicken broth. Cover and simmer until tender; remove from heat.

Pour into electric blender and purée. Return to soup pot and add remaining chicken broth, pumpkin, heavy cream and sherry. Stir and return to heat. Add salt and pepper to taste. Serve with a sprinkle of nutmeg on top of each serving.

Roast Goose with Port Giblet Gravy

1 whole goose, 12 to 14
  pounds
3 cups water
1 medium onion, sliced
1 large carrot
1 celery stalk, including
  leaves
5 to 6 whole peppercorns
Freshly ground pepper

1 or 2 lemons, halved
Fresh rosemary and
  parsley sprigs
1 tablespoon butter
Salt and pepper
3 tablespoons all-purpose
  flour
1 cup Port (we suggest
  tawny Port)

Remove neck and giblets from goose, and set aside liver. Place giblets in medium saucepan with water, onion, carrot, celery, salt and peppercorns. Bring to boil, then reduce heat and simmer 1-1/2 hours, or until giblets are tender. Allow to cool. Chop and put aside, retaining cooking broth.

Preheat oven to 350 degrees.

Remove all excess fat from goose. Rinse goose and pat dry. Rub inside and out with lemon halves and sprinkle cavity with salt to taste. Place rosemary and parsley in cavity. Truss goose and skewer opening. Place breast side up on rack in large roasting pan. With two-tine fork, prick skin in several places to drain fat during roasting. Baste several times during roasting period with 2 cups of boiling water. This will help get rid of fat.

Roast goose 3 hours or until meat thermometer reaches 185 degrees and thigh meat feels soft and joint moves easily, about 16 to 20 minutes per pound. As goose cooks, remove rendered fat with bulb baster and set aside.

When goose is done, transfer to a warm platter and let stand 15 minutes. Cut liver into 4 pieces and sauté in a small amount of the butter until browned on outside but still pink within. Chop for use in gravy.

Skim fat from roasting pan, add giblet stock and bring to boil over direct heat, scraping to remove browned bits from bottom of pan. Mix the rest of the butter and flour together to form a paste and add to stock. Season to taste with salt and pepper. Add port and stir in chopped giblets and liver. Simmer until gravy thickens. Transfer to serving dish.

To serve, place goose on large platter. Garnish with parsley sprigs, small pears, apples, grapes, and lemon leaves.

Apple-Sage Dressing

7 tablespoons butter
1 cup chopped onion
1/2 cup chopped celery
6 to 8 cups cubed bread
2 cups peeled, cored, and
   diced tart apple
1 cup chopped walnuts

1/4 cup fresh parsley,
   chopped
2 eggs, beaten
2 teaspoons ground sage
1 teaspoon salt
1/2 teaspoon dried thyme
1/2 teaspoon pepper

Preheat oven to 350 degrees. Butter a baking dish.

Melt butter in skillet over medium-high heat. Add onion and celery and sauté until softened. Transfer to a large bowl and mix in the bread. Stir in remaining ingredients and blend well. Place in buttered baking dish. Cover tightly with foil. Bake 30 minutes covered. Then remove foil and bake an additional 20 minutes until top browns and begins to crisp.

Nutmeg Mashed Potatoes

10 medium baking potatoes
6 tablespoons butter or
  margarine
2/3 cup warm cream or milk

Salt and pepper
Ground nutmeg
Sliced scallions for
  garnish

Peel potatoes and cut into quarters. Cook in boiling, salted water about 30 minutes or until tender. Drain well and put through a food mill or ricer, or mash with potato masher.

With an electric mixer or a whisk, whip mashed potatoes, gradually adding butter and warm cream. Season to taste with salt, pepper and nutmeg. Garnish with sliced scallions.

Glazed Carrots and Parsnips

1-1/2 pounds medium
  carrots (8–9)
1-1/2 pounds medium
  parsnips (7–8)

3/4 stick butter or
  margarine
1/3 cup packed light
  brown sugar
1/2 teaspoon salt

Peel and cut carrots and parsnips in half lengthwise, then in 2 to 3-inch lengths. Bring 1 inch of water to boil in a 12-inch skillet. Add vegetables and return to boil. Reduce heat to low; cover and simmer 10 to 15 minutes until vegetables are almost tender; drain off water.

Add butter, brown sugar, and salt to carrots and parsnips in skillet. Cook over medium-high heat, gently turning vegetables occasionally, until sugar dissolves and vegetables are glazed and golden, about 10 minutes.

Spiced Red Cabbage

1 medium red cabbage,
  shredded
2 tablespoons vegetable oil
1/2 cup chopped onion
2 tart apples, quartered
  and chopped
4 tablespoons red wine
  vinegar

2 tablespoons sugar
1 bay leaf
1/2 teaspoon salt
1/4 teaspoon pepper
1/8 teaspoon ground
  cloves

Place cabbage in a large kettle of boiling salted water; boil for 1 minute. Drain. Return to kettle; stir in remaining ingredients. Cover and simmer for 1 hour or until cabbage is tender. Remove bay leaf.

Fresh Cranberry Relish

1 12-ounce package fresh
  cranberries
1/4 cup water
1-1/2 cups sugar
1/2 cup raspberry vinegar
1/2 cup golden raisins

2 teaspoons fresh grated
  ginger
2 cups diced apples
1 teaspoon cinnamon
1/2 teaspoon nutmeg
1/4 teaspoon cloves

Simmer fresh cranberries, water, sugar and vinegar until soft, about 10 minutes. Add raisins, ginger, diced apples, cinnamon, nutmeg and cloves. Continue to cook an additional 15 minutes to blend all flavors. Cook and chill in refrigerator.

Pecan Tarts

Prepared pastry for a
  single crust pie
1 egg
1/4 cup sugar
1/8 teaspoon salt

2 tablespoons butter,
  melted
1/3 cup corn syrup
1/2 cup pecan halves or
  pieces

Preheat oven to 375 degrees.

Prepare pastry for one pie crust as directed on package. Fold crust until you get eight sections. Cut and form each into balls, then roll out into 4-inch circles. Gently mold into pastry-lined muffin pans, pleating as necessary.

In a mixing bowl, beat egg, sugar, salt, butter and syrup thoroughly. Add nuts. Pour into muffin cups.

Bake 35 minutes or until pastry is light brown. Cool, place in airtight plastic bag and store until ready to serve. Makes 8 small 4-inch tarts.

Apple and Mince Tart

Pastry for a single crust
  pie (see note)
3 large cooking apples
Juice of 1 lemon
1-1/2 cups prepared
  mincemeat

2 tablespoons sugar
Cinnamon
Nutmeg
2 teaspoons butter
1/2 cup apricot preserves
  (optional)

Preheat oven to 375 degrees.

Peel and core 3 large tart cooking apples. Cut in thin slices and toss with juice of 1 lemon. Spread the mincemeat in the unbaked pie shell. Top with two layers of overlapping apple slices. Sprinkle each layer with 1 tablespoon sugar, and ground cinnamon and nutmeg to taste; dot with 2 teaspoons butter.

Bake tart 55 to 60 minutes until crust is golden and apples are tender. Remove from oven and, if using, glaze with 1/2 cup melted and strained apricot preserves. Serve with vanilla ice cream, if desired.

Note: Purchase a refrigerated pie shell, or use your favorite pie pastry recipe.

Southwest Christmas Dinner
For Eight

Cool Cucumber Soup
Turkey Southwest Style - Chili Gravy
Sage Cornbread Stuffing
Mashed Potatoes - Acorn Squash with Sausage
Peppery Succotash
Jicama-Orange Salad
Cornmeal Biscuits
Bourbon Pecan Pie
Coffee - Tea

The Wines

Serving several wines with this dinner? If so, we suggest a white wine such as a Chardonnay or Sauvignon Blanc to accompany the soup and salad. The turkey, with its sage and cornbread stuffing, really calls for a red wine such as a Petit Syrah (Shiraz), a young Merlot or a Sangiovese.

If, however, you want to serve just one wine for this dinner, you have a choice of a good Chardonnay, or the Petit Syrah...and if Petit Syrah is not available (it is still in limited production), then go with the Merlot.

A Late Harvest Gewürztraminer or Late Harvest Zinfandel would be excellent choices for serving with the Bourbon Pecan Pie...and sipping afterward, too.

Cool Cucumber Soup

4 medium cucumbers
2-1/2 cups buttermilk
1 teaspoon salt

1/4 teaspoon pepper
2 teaspoons instant
    minced onion

Wash one cucumber but do not pare; cut 4 to 6 thin slices and reserve for garnish. Pare remaining cucumbers and cut cucumbers into 3/4-inch slices.

Pour 1/4 cup of the buttermilk into blender container; add half the cucumber slices and blend on high speed until smooth. Add remaining slices, salt, pepper, and onion. Blend until smooth, about 1 minute. Stir in remaining buttermilk. Chill. Serve in cups and garnish each with reserved cucumber slice.

This soup may be made a day or two in advance and refrigerated.

Turkey Southwest Style with Sage Cornbread Stuffing and Chili Gravy

1 whole turkey, 12 to 14 pounds
1 cup chopped onion
3/4 cup chopped celery
1/2 cup butter
3 cups cornbread stuffing mix
1 cup chicken broth
1 cup corn (fresh, frozen or canned)
1 can (4 ounces) diced green chiles
1/2 cup chopped toasted walnuts
1 egg, lightly beaten
2-1/2 teaspoons dried sage
Salt and pepper

Preheat oven to 325 degrees.

Rinse turkey, pat dry. Put aside. Sauté onion and celery in 1/4 cup of the butter until soft. Combine with stuffing mix, broth, corn, 1/4 cup of the chiles, nuts, egg, 1 teaspoon of the sage and pepper to taste. Mix well, spoon into turkey cavity and truss. Melt the remaining 1/4 cup of butter, add 1/2 teaspoon of the sage, and brush over the turkey.

Roast for 3 to 3 1/2 hours, until meat thermometer registers 170 degrees in breast or 180 degrees in thigh. Let stand 20 minutes before carving; reserve drippings for chili gravy.

CHILI GRAVY:
Pour fat and drippings from turkey pan into 4-cup measure. Skim off and reserve 1/3 cup fat. Discard remaining fat, reserving drippings. Add broth to drippings to measure 4 cups. Melt reserved fat in saucepan; stir in 1/2 cup flour

until smooth. Cook 2 minutes, stirring. Gradually add broth, remaining chilies, remaining sage, and dash of pepper. Bring to boil. Reduce heat; simmer, covered, until thickened slightly, about 5 minutes.

Garlic Mashed Potatoes

12 medium baking
  potatoes
6 tablespoons butter or
  margarine
2 large cloves garlic, minced

2/3 cup warm cream or
  milk
Salt and pepper
2 tablespoons fresh
  parsley, minced

Peel potatoes and cut into quarters. Cook in boiling, salted water for about 30 minutes or until tender. Drain well and put through a food mill or ricer, or mash with potato masher. Do not use a food processor.

In a small skillet, melt 2 tablespoons butter. Sauté garlic at low heat, stirring often until soft but not browned, about 5 minutes. Put aside.

With electric mixer or whisk, whip mashed potatoes, gradually adding garlic butter, butter and cream. Season to taste with salt and pepper. Mix in minced parsley.

Acorn Squash with Sausage

4 small acorn squash
8 tablespoons pure maple
  syrup

4 tablespoons butter or
  margarine
1/2 pound bulk hot Italian
  sausage

Preheat oven to 350 degrees. Cut squash in half; clean seeds from cavity. Put an eighth of the syrup, butter and sausage in each squash cavity. Place on a baking sheet. Bake for 30 to 40 minutes or until squash is fork-tender.

Peppery Succotash

2 to 3 tablespoons butter
  or margarine
1 green bell pepper,
  seeded and diced
1 red bell pepper, seeded
  and diced

3/4 cup thinly sliced
  scallions
2 packages (10 ounces
  each) frozen succotash
1 cup water
Salt and ground pepper

In large saucepan over medium heat, melt the butter. Add diced peppers and 1/2 cup of scallions; sauté 2 minutes. Add succotash and water; bring to a boil. Cover, reduce heat to medium and simmer 5 to 7 minutes until beans are tender.

Sprinkle remaining scallions over succotash; season with salt and pepper to taste.

Jicama-Orange Salad

2 medium oranges, peeled with a knife to remove white membrane, then thinly sliced
3/4 pound jicama (1 small root or a piece), peeled and cut into 1/4-inch julienne sticks (about 4 cups)

1/4 cup fresh orange juice
2 tablespoons fresh lime juice
1 to 2 tablespoons fresh cilantro leaves
Butter lettuce leaves (1 head)
Mustard vinaigrette (recipe follows)

Combine oranges and jicama. (At this point, you can cover and chill overnight.)

Mix orange juice with lime juice and pour over the salad; then sprinkle with the cilantro. Serve on butter lettuce leaves with mustard vinaigrette.

MUSTARD VINAIGRETTE:

2 teaspoons each Dijon mustard and finely chopped red onion

2 tablespoons distilled white vinegar
1/3 cup salad oil

Whisk together mustard, onion, vinegar, and salad oil.

Cornmeal Biscuits

3 cups flour
1 cup cornmeal
8 teaspoons baking
  powder
4 teaspoons sugar
1 teaspoon cream of
  tartar

1 teaspoon salt
1/2 teaspoon ground sage
1 cup vegetable shortening
1-1/3 cups milk

Preheat oven to 450 degrees.

Stir together flour, cornmeal, baking powder, sugar, cream of tartar, salt, and sage. Cut in shortening until mixture resembles coarse crumbs. Make a well in the center; add milk all at once. Stir just until dough clings together.

Knead gently on a lightly floured surface for 10 to 12 strokes. Roll or pat to a 1/2-inch thickness. Cut with a 2-1/2-inch biscuit cutter, dipping cutter in flour between cuts. Transfer to an ungreased baking sheet. Bake for 10 to 12 minutes or until golden. Serve warm.

Bourbon Pecan Pie

Pastry for a single crust
  pie (see note)
1 cup light or dark corn
  syrup
1/2 cup sugar

4 tablespoons butter or
  margarine, melted
3 lightly beaten eggs
2 tablespoons Bourbon
2 cups pecan halves
Whipped cream (optional)

Preheat oven to 400 degrees.

In mixing bowl, combine corn syrup, sugar, and melted butter. Stir in eggs, Bourbon, and pecan halves. Pour mixture into unbaked pie shell. Bake 15 minutes; reduce oven temperature to 350 degrees and bake about 30 minutes longer.

Serve with lightly sweetened whipped cream, if using.

Note: Purchase a refrigerated pie shell, or use your favorite pie pastry recipe.

Traditional Chanukah Celebration
For Eight

Borscht
Red and Green Coleslaw Salad
Brisket of Beef
Spiced Carrots - Tiny Peas with Mint
Potato and Parsnip Latkes
with Applesauce and Sour Cream
Apple Strudel
Nuts - Surprise Gelt - Fruit
Coffee - Tea

The Wines

There are two schools of thought on what are considered appropriate wines for this celebration.

One inisists that the only wines that are right are Riesling and Chenin Blanc.

The other is equally insistent that the only wines to be served with a Chanukah Celebration should be a Pinot Noir or a Merlot.

We've tried both. Liked both. So it is up to you. We suggest that the wisdom of the ages prevail: Serve the Riesling or Chenin Blanc <u>and</u> the Pinot Noir or Merlot.

The only thing we will add is that a Late Harvest Gewürztraminer will be very enjoyable with the apple strudel and while the children open their gelt.

Borscht

3 bunches beets (approximately 2 pounds)
3 medium onions
1 tablespoon salad oil
4 vegetable bouillon cubes
3 to 4 large carrots, peeled and coarsely shredded

6 medium potatoes (approximately 2 pounds)
1/4 cup lemon juice
3 tablespoons sugar
1 teaspoon salt

Peel and cut beets into 1/4-inch pieces. Slice onions into thin slices.

Heat salad oil in a 5 quart Dutch oven over medium heat, add onions, and sauté until translucent, about 10 minutes. Add beets, bouillon cubes, and 3 quarts of water, heat to boiling, then reduce heat to low and simmer for 30 minutes. Add carrots, simmer for 15 minutes or until carrots are tender. Cover, cool and refrigerate.

In a 3-quart pan, add potatoes to boiling water, reduce heat to low and simmer for 30 minutes or until potatoes are tender. Drain, cool, peel, and dice into 1/4-inch squares. Refrigerate.

When ready to serve, add lemon juice, sugar and salt to borscht. Heat, and pour over 7 or 8 potato cubes in each soup bowl.

Red and Green Coleslaw Salad

1 medium head of green
  cabbage
1 medium head of red
  cabbage
1 medium red onion
1/2 cup mayonnaise
1/4 cup cider vinegar

1/2 teaspoon sugar
3 tablespoons Dijon
  mustard
1/2 teaspoon salt
1/3 teaspoon coarsely
  ground black pepper

Quarter both cabbages, remove tough ribs, and cut into thin slices. Cut onion in half lengthwise, cut into thin slices, and then cut in half. Combine onions and cabbage.

In a separate bowl, mix mayonnaise, vinegar, sugar, mustard, salt, and pepper. Add to cabbage mixture; mix well. Refrigerate until ready to serve.

Brisket of Beef

4 pounds lean brisket of beef

Salt and black pepper

2 medium yellow onions, peeled and coarsely chopped

1/2 cup celery, chopped

1/4 cup fresh parsley

3 cups beef broth

Juice of 1 lemon

3 to 4 whole cloves

1/2 teaspoon ground cinnamon

3 pounds sweet potatoes, peeled and quartered

6 medium carrots, peeled and cut into 2-inch pieces

12 ounces pitted prunes

1 tablespoon honey

2 tablespoons white vinegar

Preheat oven to 475 degrees.

Lightly salt and pepper the brisket of beef and place meat on a rack in a large roasting pan. Brown the meat, fatty side up, in the oven for 30 minutes. Remove the meat and the rack, set aside. Add the onions, celery, and parsley to the roasting pan. Place the brisket of beef on top of the vegetables, without the rack. Add the beef broth, lemon juice, cloves and cinnamon, and cover pan.

Reduce oven temperature to 300 degrees, and bake the brisket for 2-1/2 hours. Remove the pan from the oven, and add sweet potatoes, carrots, and the prunes. Mix honey with the vinegar and pour over meat, return the covered pan to oven and bake for 1 hour more. Slice the meat and serve with the vegetables and sauce from the pan.

Spiced Carrots

3 cups carrots, cut in thin
  strips
1 cup pineapple juice
3/4 teaspoon ground
  cinnamon

1/8 teaspoon ground
  nutmeg
Sprinkling of black
  pepper

In a saucepan, combine carrots, pineapple juice, cinnamon, nutmeg and pepper. Bring to a boil. Reduce heat to simmer. Cook, covered, about 15 minutes until carrots are crisp-tender.

Tiny Peas with Mint

2 tablespoons vegetable oil
1 cup onion, diced
1-1/2 teaspoons grated
  lemon zest

2 10-ounce boxes frozen
  tiny peas, thawed
Salt and pepper to taste
1 tablespoon fresh mint,
  chopped

In a medium saucepan, heat oil over low heat. Add the onion and lemon zest; cook gently, stirring occasionally, until onion is soft but not browned, about 4 minutes.

Add the peas to the pot; stir to combine thoroughly. Season with salt and pepper and cook, stirring, for about 5 minutes, or until the peas are heated through. Stir in mint and serve immediately.

Potato and Parsnip Latkes

2 pounds potatoes
1 pound parsnips
2 green onions
1/4 cup all-purpose flour

1 teaspoon salt
1/4 teaspoon black pepper
2 large eggs, beaten
Salad oil

Peel and finely shred the potatoes and parsnips, squeezing excess water from them. Add chopped green onions, flour, salt, pepper, and eggs to mixture; combine thoroughly.

Heat 4 tablespoons of oil in 12-inch skillet over medium heat. Drop 1/4 cup of the mixture into skillet and flatten to 3 or 4 inches in diameter. Brown each side for about 5 minutes. Place on wire rack to drain. Refrigerate between sheets of wax paper until ready to serve. To reheat, place latkes on a wire rack on a cookie sheet and heat in oven at 375 degrees for about 10 minutes.

Applesauce

2 pounds tart cooking
  apples, peeled and sliced
1 cup sugar

1/4 pound seedless grapes,
  cleaned
1/2 teaspoon ground
  cinnamon

Place apples in medium pan. Add 1 cup water, bring to a boil, cover. Simmer for 8 to 10 minutes, stirring often. Add sugar, mixing thoroughly. Mash apples with potato masher. Add grapes. Bring to a boil, adding water if necessary. Remove, cool and store in refrigerator. Serve cool.

Apple Strudel

1 cup flour
1/2 teaspoon salt
1 egg, slightly beaten
2 tablespoons vegetable
  oil
4 tablespoons warm water
3 tablespoons seedless
  raisins
3 tablespoons currants
2/3 cup confectioners'
  sugar

1/2 teaspoon ground
  cinnamon
2 pounds cooking apples,
  peeled, cored and
  coarsely grated
3 tablespoons butter,
  melted
1/4 pound ground
  almonds
Confectioners' sugar for
  decorating

Lightly oil a baking sheet. Combine flour and salt in a large bowl. Make a well in the center and pour in the egg and oil.

Add the water slowly, stirring with a fork, to make a soft, sticky dough. Work the dough in the bowl until it leaves the sides of the bowl. Then place on a lightly floured surface and gently knead for 12 to 15 minutes.

Form the dough into a ball, place it on a cloth and cover it with a warmed bowl. Let it rest in a warm place for an hour. Put the raisins, currants, sugar, cinnamon, and apples into a bowl and mix very thoroughly.

With a warm rolling pin, roll the dough on a clean, lightly floured, cotton cloth to a 1/8-inch thickness, turning and lifting to prevent its sticking to the cloth.

Gently stretch the dough until it is paper thin, then trim to about 24 inches by 27 inches. Let it rest for 15 minutes.

Preheat oven to 375 degrees.

Place the dough with one of the long sides towards you, brush with melted butter and sprinkle with ground almonds. Spread the apple mixture evenly over the dough, leaving a 2-inch border all around. Fold the border in over the apple mixture. Gently lift the corners of the cloth nearest to you and begin to roll up the strudel. Stop after each turn and pat it into shape. Slide it onto the prepared baking sheet, and brush with melted butter.

Bake for about 40 minutes until golden brown. Decorate with confectioners' sugar. Slice, and serve hot or cold.

Surprise Gelt

12 ounces dried apricots
1/4 pound walnut halves
1/4 pound toasted
** almonds**

1/4 pound semi-sweet
** chocolate**
Gold foil squares (see
** note)**

Steam apricots for 15 minutes until they are plump. Cool and stuff each apricot with a walnut half, a toasted almond, or a small piece of chocolate. Wrap individually in gold foil. (May be made a week or two in advance, stored in an airtight container in refrigerator, and left at room temperature the day of celebration.)

Note: Gold foil squares are available at candy supply and craft stores.

Festive New Year's Dinner
For Eight

Sherried Carrot Soup
Hearts of Palm Salad
Cornish Game Hens with Fruit and Nut Stuffing
Dilled Cucumber Sauté - Sweet Potato Puff
Dried Fruit Chutney
Parker House Rolls
Raspberry Vanilla Ice Cream Swirl
Spicy Chocolate Macaroons
Coffee - Tea

The Wines

The obvious choice of wine for this day is Champagne, but here are some suggestions for wines to enhance the dinner menu and serving the Champagne later in the evening.

In white wines, Chardonnay is our first choice, and we suggest a Chardonnay that is relatively young, with little oakiness. A close second would be Pinot Blanc, which has slightly less body, but would be excellent with this menu.

Our first choice in red wines is a classic Cabernet Sauvignon. For those who like a little less body to the wine, and are afficionados of Merlot, this is an ideal menu for it.

Champagne (Sparkling Wine) is a good choice to accompany dessert and for evening drinking on this festive occasion.

Please note, in choosing your wines to accompany dinner that some people have a problem with mixing red wines with white wines. Since Champagne is a white wine, you may want to consider this in your dinner wine selection, if the evening is going to include Champagne.

Sherried Carrot Soup

1 onion, chopped
3 tablespoons butter
8 carrots, peeled and cut
   into 1/4-inch-thick slices
1/4 teaspoon ground
   ginger
1/2 teaspoon ground
   cinnamon

5-1/2 cups chicken broth
1/2 cup medium-dry
   sherry
1-1/2 cups heavy cream
White pepper
Chopped fresh parsley
   leaves for garnish

In a kettle, cook the onion in the butter over moderately low heat, stirring until the onion is softened. Add the carrots, the ginger, and the cinnamon, and cook the mixture, stirring, for 1 minute.

Add the broth and bring the mixture to a boil. Simmer, stirring occasionally, for 20 minutes, or until the carrots are very tender. In a blender or food processor purée the mixture in batches, transferring it to the kettle as it is puréed. Add the sherry and the cream. Bring the soup to a boil and simmer for 5 minutes.

Season the soup with salt and white pepper to taste. Garnish with parsley.

Hearts of Palm Salad

2 tablespoons fresh lemon
  juice
2-1/2 teaspoons Dijon
  mustard
1 clove garlic, finely
  minced
6 tablespoons olive oil
1 can (14 ounces) hearts
  of palm, drained and
  sliced into rounds
1 can (14 ounces)
  artichoke hearts,
  drained and quartered
1-1/2 heads butter lettuce
16 cherry tomatoes,
  halved

Combine the lemon juice, mustard, and garlic in a medium bowl. Gradually whisk in olive oil. Season dressing to taste with salt and pepper. Add hearts of palm and artichoke hearts. Let marinate at room temperature at least 20 minutes and up to 4 hours, tossing occasionally.

Line 8 plates with lettuce leaves. Using a slotted spoon, divide the hearts of palm and artichoke hearts among the plates. Garnish with tomatoes. Spoon remaining dressing over salad and serve.

Cornish Game Hens with Fruit and Nut Stuffing

8 Cornish hens (1 pound each)
1/2 teaspoon salt
1-3/4 cups apricot nectar
3 tablespoons apricot jam
3 tablespoons light brown sugar
6 whole cloves
1/2 teaspoon ground cinnamon
4 tablespoons dry white wine
1-1/2 teaspoons cornstarch
Fruit and Nut Stuffing (recipe follows)

Preheat oven to 425 degrees. Wash hens; dry with absorbent paper. Salt hens inside and out and set aside. Prepare stuffing. Stuff hens. Fasten skin with skewers; tie legs securely. Place on a rack of a baking pan.

Combine nectar, jam, brown sugar, cloves, and cinnamon in a pot. Boil, stirring constantly. Combine wine and cornstarch; stir into nectar mixture. Cook until thick and smooth. Baste hens. Roast for 1 hour, basting continuously.

Fruit and Nut Stuffing

3 cups fine dry bread crumbs
6 tablespoons butter, melted
1 cup coarsely chopped dried fruit
1 cup chopped pecans or walnuts
3/4 teaspoon dried rosemary leaves
3/4 teaspoon dried thyme
1-1/2 teaspoons salt

In a large bowl, combine bread crumbs and melted butter. Add dried fruit, nuts and seasonings. Mix well before stuffing.

Dilled Cucumber Sauté

3 cucumbers (8 inches
  each), peeled
2 tablespoons butter or
  margarine
2 tablespoons all-purpose
  flour
3/4 cup half-and-half

2 tablespoons dried dill
  weed
1 teaspoon granulated
  sugar
1/2 teaspoon salt
Dash white pepper

Cut peeled cucumbers in half lengthwise and scrape out
seeds with spoon. Cut cucumbers in 1/2-inch cubes. Sauté
in butter in large, heavy pan until tender but still firm, about
2 minutes. Sprinkle with flour and stir to blend. Add half-
and-half, dill, sugar, salt and pepper.

Cook over moderate heat until thickened, stirring constantly.
If serving is delayed and sauce becomes too thick, add a little
more half-and-half.

Sweet Potato Puff

2 cans (16 ounces each)
sweet potatoes in light
syrup, drained
3 eggs, separated
1 cup half-and-half or
light cream
2 tablespoons all-purpose
flour

2 tablespoons brown
sugar
1 teaspoon salt
1/4 teaspoon ground
nutmeg
1/4 teaspoon ground
cinnamon
1/4 teaspoon ground
pepper

Preheat oven to 400 degrees.

In a food processor, combine the potatoes, egg yolks, cream, flour, brown sugar, salt, and the spices. Pulse on and off until mixture is fairly smooth. In a large bowl with electric mixer on high speed, beat egg whites until stiff, but not dry. Gently fold potato mixture into beaten egg whites.

Spoon or pour mixture into a buttered 1-quart baking dish. Place dish in a pan of hot water and bake 15 minutes. Reduce oven temperature to 350 degrees and bake about 25 minutes longer or until puffed and golden on top. Serve immediately.

Dried Fruit Chutney

1/2 pound dried apricots, chopped

1/2 cup raisins

1/2 cup dried pineapple or other sweet dried fruit, chopped

1/2 cup preserved, candied ginger, chopped

1 cup sweet onion, diced

1-1/4 cups cider vinegar

1-1/4 cups dark brown sugar

1 teaspoon salt

1 teaspoon dry mustard

1/2 teaspoon black pepper

1/4 teaspoon turmeric

Grated rind and juice of 1 orange

1/4 cup toasted walnuts, chopped

Combine all the ingredients together in a large steel or glass pan and bring to a boil. Reduce the flame and keep at a simmer until the chutney has thickened. Stir occasionally to prevent scorching. If more liquid is needed, add orange juice. Just before serving, stir in walnuts.

Serve chilled or at room temperature. May be made ahead and stored in refrigerator.

Raspberry Vanilla Ice Cream Swirl

4 baskets (1/2 pint each) raspberries, or 2 packages frozen raspberries, thawed
3/4 cup sugar

2 tablespoons fresh lemon juice
3 pints vanilla ice cream, softened

Blend berries, sugar, and lemon juice in a food processor until berries are coarsely chopped. Transfer to a bowl. Cover and let stand 2 to 6 hours at room temperature. Add ice cream to berry sauce; fold together. Scoop into bowls. Serve with Spicy Chocolate Macaroons.

Spicy Chocolate Macaroons

1-1/2 cups coconut flakes
1/2 cup sugar
2 squares unsweetened chocolate, melted
3 tablespoons flour

1/8 teaspoon salt
1 teaspoon cinnamon
1/2 teaspoon nutmeg
1 teaspoon vanilla
2 egg whites

Combine coconut, sugar, flour, salt, cinnamon and nutmeg in a bowl and mix. Stir in chocolate, egg whites and vanilla. Mix well.

Drop from teaspoon on lightly greased baking sheets.

Bake at 325 degrees for 20 to 25 minutes, or until edges brown. Remove from baking sheets. Makes about 18 to 20.

Southern New Year's Dinner
For Eight

Corn Chowder
Herbed Roast Chicken with Gravy
Quick Hoppin' John
Green Bean Almond Sauté
Orange Sweet Potato Casserole
Cranberry Mold with Grapes
Tomatoes with Tarragon
Pecan Biscuits
Classic Coconut Pie with Vanilla Ice Cream
Coffee - Tea

The Wines

Semillion and Viognier are our suggestions for the white wines for this menu, but because they are in limited production, you may not be able to find them. A Chardonnay will be very satisfactory, as will a Sauvignon Blanc.

In a red wine, Petit Syrah is suggested, as are a Gamay (also known as Gamay Beaujolais) or a Grenache.

A Muscat Canelli (Muscat) will be a nice touch to serve with dessert.

One note: If you are celebrating the New Year with Champagne, you may want to serve the white wines with this menu. Some people prefer not to mix red and white wines.

Corn Chowder

1 large white onion, diced
1 stalk celery, diced
2 carrots, peeled and diced
3 strips of smoked bacon, diced
3 tablespoons corn oil
2 cloves minced garlic
1 cup white wine
6 ears of fresh corn, removed from the cobs, or 3 cups frozen corn, thawed
3 cups chicken broth
2 cups cream
2 tablespoons fresh thyme, chopped
2 tablespoons fresh basil, chopped
Salt and pepper
Tabasco

Sauté onions, celery, carrots, and bacon with corn oil until soft.

Add garlic and cook approximately 1 minute. Add white wine and cook 3 minutes over medium heat. Add corn, chicken broth, cream, and thyme. Cook until tender. Add basil, salt and pepper, and Tabasco to taste. Remove 1/2 of the soup, purée in processor or blender and add back to remainder of the soup.

Quick Hoppin' John

1/2 pound lean bacon
1 cup chopped onions
1 cup regular long-grain
  rice

1 can (16 ounces) black-
  eyed peas
1-2/3 cups chicken broth
  or water

In a large skillet over medium-low heat, cook bacon until crisp. Remove bacon, drain, crumble, and reserve. Pour off all but 1 tablespoon bacon drippings from pan. Add onion and sauté about 5 minutes or until translucent.

Stir in rice, undrained peas, and broth. Cover and simmer 20 to 30 minutes until rice is tender. Add reserved crumbled bacon and toss to combine; serve warm.

Note: This dish is essential in a Southern New Year's dinner. Legend has it that in the coming year you will get a dollar for every black-eyed pea that you eat on New Year's Day.

Green Bean Almond Sauté

2 pounds green beans
2 tablespoons olive oil

1/4 teaspoon black pepper
1/2 cup sliced almonds

About 30 minutes before serving, trim ends from green beans. In a 5-quart pan over high heat, heat green beans and enough water to cover to boiling. Reduce heat to medium-low; simmer 5 to 10 minutes until green beans are tender-crisp. Drain.

In same pan over medium heat, heat olive oil and add green beans, almonds and pepper. Stir occasionally until beans are tender and begin to brown.

Herbed Roast Chicken
with Gravy

1 whole chicken (5 to 7 pounds)

4 scallions

3 tablespoons butter or margarine, softened

1 tablespoon minced fresh sage leaves, or 1 teaspoon dried sage

1 tablespoon minced fresh thyme leaves or 1 teaspoon dried thyme

2 tablespoons all-purpose flour

2 cups chicken broth or 1 cup each chicken broth and light cream

Preheat oven to 350 degrees.

Remove giblets from chicken and set aside. Rinse chicken inside and out and pat dry. In food processor, combine scallions, butter, sage, and thyme. Pulse on and off several times to form a paste. Rub mixture inside and outside of chicken, placing any remaining mixture in chicken cavity. Roast for 2 to 2 1/2 hours (15 to 20 minutes per pound) until juices run clear, and there is no hint of pink when thigh is pierced. Remove chicken to serving platter and keep warm.

To prepare gravy, pour pan juices into a heatproof measuring cup. Skim off 3 tablespoons clear yellow drippings from top of juices and return to roasting pan. Discard remaining clear drippings from measuring cup, reserving degreased juices for gravy; add enough chicken broth to make 2-1/2 cups total liquid. Stir flour into roasting pan over medium heat 4 to 5 minutes until well browned. Gradually stir in broth mixture; simmer 3 to 4 minutes until gravy is thickened, stirring occasionally.

Orange Sweet Potato Casserole

3 pounds medium sweet
  potatoes or yams
1/3 cup half-and-half
1/4 cup (1/2 stick) butter,
  at room temperature
1/2 cup orange marmalade

2 large eggs, beaten to
  blend
3/4 teaspoon ground
  allspice
1/2 teaspoon ground
  cinnamon
Toasted pecans

Butter an 8-inch glass baking dish with 2-inch high sides. Place potatoes in a large saucepan; cover with water and bring to a boil over medium-high heat. Cover partially and cook until potatoes are very soft, about 1 hour. Drain potatoes. Peel and trim.

Preheat oven to 350 degrees.

Place potatoes in a food processor, add all remaining ingredients except pecans and a few teaspoons of butter. Process until mixture is smooth. Transfer mixture to prepared baking dish. Dot mixture with remaining butter.

Bake soufflé until center is set and top begins to brown, about 50 minutes. Garnish with pecans.

Cranberry Mold with Grapes

2 cups boiling water
2 packages (3 ounces
   each) raspberry-flavored
   gelatin
2 cans (16 ounces each)
   whole cranberry sauce

1 can (13 1/2 ounces)
   crushed pineapple
12 small bunches seedless
   green grapes, washed
   and drained

Pour boiling water over gelatin, stirring until gelatin is dissolved. Add cranberry sauce and the pineapple with its syrup. Stir until mixed thoroughly. Pour into a 2-quart ring mold; chill until firm.

Unmold onto a large serving plate. Place bunches of grapes in center of mold and around edge.

Tomatoes with Tarragon

8 large tomatoes, sliced
1/2 cup olive oil
1/2 cup balsamic vinegar

1 bunch fresh tarragon,
   stemmed

Arrange tomatoes on platter. Drizzle oil, then vinegar over tomatoes. Season with salt and pepper. Sprinkle with tarragon or make individual salad plates.

Pecan Biscuits

2-1/2 cups flour
2 tablespoons sugar
1 teaspoon grated orange
  peel
1/2 teaspoon baking soda
1/2 teaspoon salt

1/2 cup chilled butter, cut
  into pieces
1 cup pecans, toasted and
  chopped
1 cup buttermilk
Additional buttermilk

Preheat oven to 425 degrees.

Combine the flour, sugar, orange peel, baking soda, and salt in large bowl. Add butter and blend with fingertips until the mixture resembles coarse meal. Mix in pecans and 1 cup buttermilk. Stir just until dough forms.

Transfer dough to floured surface and pat to 3/4-inch thick circle. Cut into rounds, using 2-inch diameter biscuit cutter. Transfer to ungreased baking sheets. Brush tops of biscuits with buttermilk. Bake until golden brown, about 18 minutes.

Classic Coconut Pie

Pastry for a single crust
  pie (see note)
1/2 cup butter
1-1/4 cups sugar
3 eggs, beaten
4 teaspoons fresh lemon
  juice

1 teaspoon vanilla extract
1-1/4 cups sweetened
  shredded coconut
Vanilla ice cream (optional)
Whipped cream (optional)

Preheat oven to 450 degrees.

Press the crust into 9-inch glass pie plate. Trim and crimp edges. Bake crust until light golden, about 9 minutes. Transfer to rack and cool. Reduce oven temperature to 350 degrees.

Melt butter in heavy medium saucepan over low heat. Add sugar and stir just until mixture is heated through. Transfer to a bowl. Add eggs, lemon juice, and vanilla and whisk to combine. Stir in the coconut.

Pour filling into the crust. Bake until filling is deep golden brown and set, about 40 minutes. Cool on a rack.

This pie can be made one day ahead. Cover and chill. Bring to room temperature before serving. Serve with vanilla ice cream or whipped cream.

Note: Purchase a refrigerated pie shell, or use your favorite pie pastry recipe.

Elegant Easter Dinner
For Eight

Spring Green Salad
with
Orange and Sweet Onions

Baked Ham with Honey Apricot Glaze
Apricot-Ginger Relish
Spicy Mashed Sweet Potatoes
Minted Peas
Chocolate Apricot Torte
Sugared Pecans
Coffee - Tea

The Wines

Riesling, also known as Johannisberg Riesling, is the first choice for this menu. It has a light, airy taste that marries perfectly with the salad and the baked ham with the honey and apricot glaze. A second choice in white wine would be either a Chenin Blanc or a Gewürztraminer...but we believe you would be happier with the Riesling.

If a red wine is desired, it should be a light one, such as a Gamay (also known as Gamay Beaujolais), a Grenache, or a young Merlot.

To make an exciting ending, serve a dry Champagne with the Chocolate Apricot Torte.

Spring Green Salad with Orange and Sweet Onions

8 cups mixed young spring greens

1 tablespoon fresh basil, chopped

1 tablespoon fresh tarragon, chopped

1/2 cup sweet onion (such as Vidalia), thinly sliced

4 oranges, peeled with pith removed

1/4 cup sliced almonds, toasted

Orange Vinaigrette dressing (recipe below)

ORANGE VINAIGRETTE DRESSING:

1/2 teaspoon orange zest, minced

4 tablespoons fresh orange juice

1 tablespoon balsamic vinegar

1/2 teaspoon salt

1/4 teaspoon black pepper

6 tablespoons light olive oil

Combine all vinaigrette ingredients in small bowl and whisk. Put aside. Chill.

Arrange greens on 8 plates. Sprinkle with basil and tarragon. Cut orange segments in bite-size pieces and place around greens. Top greens with onion slices and drizzle with dressing. Top with sliced almonds.

Spicy Mashed Sweet Potatoes

6 to 8 large sweet potatoes, scrubbed

4 tablespoons butter, melted

1/2 teaspoon ground cinnamon

1/4 teaspoon freshly ground nutmeg

1 cup coffee cream or whole milk

1 teaspoon salt

Black pepper to taste

2 teaspoons balsamic vinegar (raspberry vinegar may be substituted)

Preheat oven to 400 degrees. Bake sweet potatoes about 50 minutes, until soft when tested with a fork. Cool and peel. Place in pan and mash. Add melted butter, cinnamon and nutmeg. Stir in cream.

Return to medium heat and beat with spoon until creamy. Season with salt, pepper and vinegar.

Minted Peas

2 tablespoons butter

1 cup onion, diced

1-1/2 teaspoons lemon zest, grated

2 10-ounce boxes frozen tiny peas, thawed

Salt and pepper to taste

1 tablespoon fresh mint, chopped

In a medium saucepan, melt butter over low heat. Add the onion and lemon zest; cook gently, stirring occasionally, until onion is soft but not browned, about 4 minutes.

Add the peas to the pot; stir to combine thoroughly. Season with salt and pepper and cook, stirring, for about 5 minutes, or until the peas are heated through. Stir in mint and serve immediately.

Baked Ham with Honey-Apricot Glaze

1 10-pound bone-in, fully-cooked smoked ham
1 cup honey
1 6-ounce can frozen orange juice concentrate, thawed
2 tablespoons mustard
2/3 cup apricot jam
1/2 teaspoon ground nutmeg
1/4 teaspoon ground cloves

Preheat oven to 325 degrees. Place ham on rack in shallow roasting pan. Mix together remaining ingredients in medium bowl; set aside. Bake ham for 30 minutes. Pour glaze over ham and continue to bake until ham is heated through, about 1 to 1-1/2 hours. Slice and serve. Ham should be refrigerated within two hours of serving.

Apricot-Ginger Relish

1 cup dried apricots, chopped
1/2 cup golden raisins
1 tablespoon fresh ginger, minced
1 teaspoon fresh orange zest
1 teaspoon fresh lemon zest
1/4 cup orange juice
1 tablespoon lemon juice
1/2 cup raspberry vinegar
1 cup apricot jam

Place chopped apricots in bowl. Cover with boiling water. Let stand 1 hour; drain. In a medium steel saucepan, combine soaked apricots, raisins, ginger, zests, orange juice, lemon juice and vinegar. Bring to a boil, stirring frequently, until apricots are tender, about 10 minutes. Add apricot jam to saucepan and combine well. Cook briefly to blend flavors and allow chutney to thicken.

Chocolate Apricot Torte

TORTE:

6 eggs, separated

1/2 cup plus 5 tablespoons
  sugar, divided

1 cup all-purpose flour

**CHOCOLATE BUTTER
CREAM:**

1/4 cup sugar

3 eggs plus 2 egg yolks

1 teaspoon vanilla extract

1 teaspoon instant coffee
  granules

2 squares (1 ounce each)
  semi-sweet chocolate

2 cups butter (no
  substitutes), softened

APRICOT FILLING:

2 cans (17 ounces each)
  apricot halves, drained

1 cup apricot preserves

Chocolate curls, optional

In a large mixing bowl, beat egg yolks and 1/2 cup sugar until thickened. In a small mixing bowl, beat egg whites until foamy. Gradually add remaining sugar, beating until stiff peaks form. Fold into yolk mixture. Gradually fold in flour. Divide batter between three greased and floured 9-inch round cake pans. Bake at 350 degrees for 15 minutes, or until golden. Cool in pans for 5 minutes; remove to wire racks to cool.

For buttercream, whisk sugar, eggs, yolks, vanilla and coffee in a saucepan. Add chocolate; cook and stir over low heat until thickened (do not boil). Cool completely. In a mixing bowl, cream butter. Gradually add chocolate mixture; set aside.

Finely chop apricots; drain and place in bowl. Stir in preserves; set aside.

Split each cake into two horizontal layers; place one on a serving plate. Spread with 2/3 cup buttercream. Top with another cake layer and 2/3 cup apricot filling. Repeat layers twice. Cover and refrigerate 3 hours before serving.

Garnish with chocolate curls if desired.

Sugared Pecans

1 egg white	1 teaspoon salt
1 tablespoon water	1 teaspoon cinnamon
1 cup sugar	1 pound pecan halves

Beat egg white and water until frothy. Mix sugar, salt and cinnamon. Dip pecan halves into egg white mixture; roll in sugar mixture. Place in shallow pan. Bake at 300 degrees for 30 to 45 minutes, stirring every 15 minutes.

May be made ahead and warmed slightly before serving.

*A Modern Passover Dinner
For Eight*

*Smoked Salmon in Endive Leaves
Spinach and Leek Soup
Roast Prime Rib
with Horseradish Crust
Sweet and Sour Red Cabbage with Raisins
Crispy Sweet Potato Patties
Steamed Asparagus with Scallion Butter
Matzo Popovers
Lemon Sponge Cake with Raspberry Glaze
Coffee - Tea*

The Wines

Chardonnay is the white wine of choice to accompany the smoked salmon, as is Chablis. Pinot Noir is the red wine that goes so well with it, too.

For the roast prime rib, a truly hearty Cabernet Sauvignon is required, with Pinot Noir as a close second choice. You may prefer serving only the Pinot Noir since it goes so well with both of these courses. For a white wine selection, you'll have to use your own discretion. We don't believe that any white wine goes well with roast beef.

With dessert, and afterwards, a late Harvest Zinfandel or a Muscat Canelli will be a great ending to this celebration.

Note: For those who prefer kosher wines for this celebration, these wines are available bearing a kosher label.

Smoked Salmon in Endive Leaves

8 ounces smoked salmon, roughly chopped

2 tablespoons olive oil

1 tablespoon fresh lemon juice

1 tablespoon fresh chives, minced

1 tablespoon chopped dill

Salt and freshly ground pepper

2 large Belgian endives

1 ounce salmon roe

In a bowl, combine smoked salmon, olive oil, lemon juice, chives, dill, salt and pepper to taste. Stir until well blended. Cover and marinate in the refrigerator for 1 hour.

Remove the outer leaves of the endives. Separate from the heart the tender leaves that are large enough for stuffing. There should be 6 to 8 leaves from each endive. Chill in the refrigerator.

At serving time, gently stir the salmon roe into the smoked salmon mixture. Spoon the salmon mixture into the endive leaves, or "boats," and arrange on individual salad plates. Serve at once.

Spinach and Leek Soup

4 tablespoons unsalted
  margarine
1/2 teaspoon garlic, minced
4 cups leeks (white and
  pale green parts only),
  chopped
6 cups chicken broth

1/2 pound fresh spinach
  (leaves only), coarsely
  chopped
Salt and pepper
1/8 teaspoon grated
  nutmeg

Melt margarine in large pot over medium heat. Sauté garlic and leeks until leeks are translucent and soft, about 15 minutes. Add broth. Cover pot and simmer until leeks are tender, about 20 minutes more.

Purée soup in small batches in food processor, adding spinach leaves to each batch. Return to pot. Season with salt and pepper. Heat soup over low heat, stirring.

Serve in bowls with a sprinkle of nutmeg on top.

Roast Prime Rib with Horseradish Crust

1 6-pound trimmed,
  boneless beef rib roast
3 cloves garlic, minced
1/4 cup olive oil
1/4 cup prepared
  horseradish

1/2 teaspoon fresh cracked
  black pepper
1/2 teaspoon salt
Salt and pepper

Preheat oven to 350 degrees. Mix garlic, oil, black pepper and horseradish in small bowl. Add salt.

Sprinkle beef roast with salt and pepper. Spread a thin layer of horseradish oil mixture on underside of roast. Place on roasting rack, underside down on rack. Spread remaining mixture over roast.

Place roast in preheated oven. Roast until meat thermometer inserted into top center of roast registers 125 degrees for rare (about 1 hour and 45 minutes). Leave roast in oven an additional length of time for medium, until thermometer registers 155 degrees.

Remove beef from oven and place roast on platter. Cover and let stand 20 minutes.

Slice beef crosswise. Serve beef with warmed pan juices drizzled over meat.

Sweet and Sour Red Cabbage with Raisins

1 large red cabbage,
  shredded
3 tablespoons vegetable
  shortening
1/2 cup onion, chopped
2 tart apples, chopped
1 teaspoon salt
1/4 cup boiling water

1/4 cup red wine
4 tablespoons tarragon
  vinegar
4 tablespoons brown
  sugar
1/4 cup raisins
1 tablespoon caraway
  seeds

Soak cabbage in cold water. Melt butter in saucepan; add onion. Simmer for 3 minutes. Add cabbage. Cover pan and simmer for 10 minutes longer. Add apples to cabbage with salt and boiling water. Cover pan and simmer for 20 minutes, or until cabbage is tender. When cabbage is tender and water absorbed, add red wine, brown sugar, raisins and caraway seeds. Simmer for 10 minutes longer. Serve hot.

Crispy Sweet Potato Patties

1-1/2 pounds sweet
   potatoes (4 to 5 medium)
2 beaten eggs
1 medium onion, chopped

1/2 teaspoon salt
1/4 teaspoon pepper
Vegetable cooking oil

Wash and peel sweet potatoes. In a food processor fitted with a medium shredding disk, coarsely shred the sweet potatoes (or shred by hand). You should have about 5 to 6 cups shredded sweet potato. In a large mixing bowl, combine shredded sweet potatoes, eggs, onion and salt.

In a large skillet, heat about 1/4 inch cooking oil over medium heat. For *each* patty, spoon about *1/4 cup* of potato mixture into the hot oil. Spread to make a circle about 3-1/2 to 4 inches in diameter. Fry patties, 2 or 3 at a time, for 1-1/2 to 2 minutes on each side, or until brown. Drain on paper towels.

To keep patties warm, arrange cooked patties in a single layer on a baking sheet; keep in a 300-degree oven, uncovered, until ready to serve.

Steamed Asparagus and Scallions with Scallion Butter

1-1/2 pounds fresh
  asparagus, trimmed
16 green scallions, trimmed
  trimmed and cut to same
  length as asparagus

2 scallions, minced
3 tablespoons unsalted
  butter

Steam asparagus and scallions over boiling water until crisp-tender, about 7 minutes. Remove and pour iced water over vegetables to stop cooking process. Put aside, keeping warm. Sauté minced scallions in butter in a small pan, about 5 minutes. Serve asparagus and 2 scallions for each person, topped with scallion butter sauce.

Matzo Popovers

2-1/4 cups water
3/4 cup vegetable
  shortening
1 teaspoon salt

1 teaspoon sugar
2-1/4 cups matzo meal
10 large eggs

In a large saucepan, bring water and shortening to boil. Add salt, sugar and matzo meal, stirring constantly with a wooden spoon until mixture pulls away from side of pan. Remove pan from heat and cool slightly. Add eggs, 1 at a time, beating with wooden spoon until smooth after each addition. Let batter rest for 30 minutes.

Preheat oven to 400 degrees and lightly grease 18 1/3-cup muffin tins. Fill muffin tins three-fourths full with batter and bake in middle of oven 45 minutes, or until popovers are golden brown and puffed. Makes 18 popovers.

Lemon Sponge Cake with Raspberry Glaze and Fresh Berries

7 large eggs, separated
1/4 teaspoon salt
1-1/2 cups sugar
1/4 cup fresh lemon juice
1 tablespoon minced lemon peel (yellow part only)
1 cup matzo cake meal
3/4 cup raspberry preserves
1 pint fresh raspberries

FOR CAKE:
Preheat oven to 350 degrees. Line bottom of 10-inch-diameter springform pan with 2-3/4-inch-high sides with parchment. Using electric mixer, beat egg whites and 1/4 teaspoon salt in large bowl until soft peaks form. Gradually add 3/4 cup sugar; beat until stiff but not dry. Using electric mixer, beat egg yolks, remaining 3/4 cup sugar, fresh lemon juice and minced lemon peel in another large bowl until beginning to thicken, about 3 minutes. Beat in matzo cake meal. Fold egg whites into yolk mixture in 2 additions.

Transfer batter to prepared pan. Bake until top is golden and toothpick inserted into center comes out clean, about 45 minutes. Cool cake in pan on rack. Run small sharp knife around pan sides to loosen cake. Release cake pan sides. Place cake on plate. Peel off parchment. (May be made 1 day ahead. Cover and let stand at room temperature.)

FOR GLAZE:
In a small saucepan, melt preserves over low heat, stirring constantly. When preserves are hot and liquid, strain through a sieve, forcing some of the berry solids and liquids into a small bowl. Pour glaze over top of cake, letting glaze run down sides of cake. Cut cake in wedges and serve on a plate with fresh raspberries.

A 4th of July Picnic
For Eight

Barbecued
Ham Patties with Pineapple Salsa
on
Toasted Kaiser Rolls

Coleslaw - Summer Potato Salad
Baked Beans

Chocolate Cherry Brownies
with
Vanilla Ice Cream & Cherry Sauce
Coffee - Iced Tea

The Wines

A Pinot Noir is our first choice for this picnic, with a Cabernet Sauvignon as a second, and a Merlot or, for a lighter wine, a Grenache. Any of these will be good.

In a white wine, the choice is a little more limited. A Riesling is our first recommendation, with a Sauvignon Blanc as a second choice. Chardonnay is also a good choice.

Whatever you serve, red, white or both, chill them. Room temperature for red wine is not 90 degrees F., it is in the low 70s...and on a hot summer day cooler is better.

Wine drinks like Sangria are another idea for this event. (See Page 142 for recipes.)

Barbecued Ham Patties
with Pineapple Salsa

1 pound lean ground
  smoked ham
1 pound lean ground loin
  of pork
2 cups bread crumbs,
  plain
1/2 teaspoon salt
1/2 teaspoon black pepper
1/2 teaspoon dried sage

1/2 cup onion, finely
  minced
1 teaspoon dried thyme
2 tablespoons Dijon
  mustard
2 eggs, beaten
Vegetable oil for brushing
  on grill rack
8 Kaiser rolls, split

AT HOME:

Mix ham, pork, bread crumbs, salt, pepper, sage, onions, thyme, mustard and eggs. Divide the meat mixture into 8 equal portions and shape into round patties, approximately 1/2-inch thick. Place on waxed paper, separated, and refrigerate until grill is ready.

In a grill with a cover, prepare a medium-hot fire for direct-heat cooking. Brush the grill rack with vegetable oil. Place the patties on the grill and cook, turning once, until done to your preference, 5 to 8 minutes on each side.

During the last few minutes of cooking, place the buns, cut side down, on the outer edges of the grill to toast lightly. Serve the burgers and toasted buns with pineapple salsa.

Pineapple Salsa

1 cup sweet onion (such as Vidalia or Walla-Walla), minced
2 tablespoons olive oil
1 10-ounce can crushed pineapple, drained (reserve juice)
1 cup brown sugar
1/2 teaspoon salt
1/4 teaspoon fresh ginger, grated
1 teaspoon fresh grated orange peel
1/2 cup raspberry vinegar
1/2 cup reserved pineapple juice

Heat olive oil in saucepan over medium heat. Sauté onions for 4 to 5 minutes until onions become soft. Add pineapple and sugar, combining onion and fruit. Add spices, mixing well. Add vinegar and pineapple juice and simmer for 15 minutes. Refrigerate until ready to use. Serve warm over ham patties.

Coleslaw

1 large head cabbage, shredded
2 medium carrots, peeled and shredded
1 teaspoon celery seed
1 cup vegetable oil
2 cups sugar
1/4 teaspoon cinnamon
1/2 cup vinegar
1 teaspoon salt
1/2 teaspoon black pepper
1 teaspoon ground mustard
1 medium onion, quartered

In a large bowl, toss cabbage, carrots and celery seed. Place the remaining ingredients in a blender or food processor; cover and process until combined. Pour over cabbage mixture and toss to coat. Cover and refrigerate for at least 2 hours or until picnic time.

Summer Potato Salad

2 pounds small red potatoes, quartered

1/2 cup crumbled blue cheese

1/2 cup plain yogurt

4 tablespoons fresh lemon juice

1/2 cup fresh basil, chopped

Salt and black pepper

4 tablespoons green onions, thinly sliced

2 tablespoons fresh parsley, chopped

White wine, if needed

Bring water to a boil in a large pot. Add potatoes and boil for 15 to 20 minutes, until tender but still firm.

While potatoes are cooking, prepare the dressing by blending the blue cheese into the yogurt. Add lemon juice and basil. Season to taste with salt and pepper. If dressing is too thick, add white wine to thin.

Pour dressing over potatoes and toss. Add green onions and parsley, tossing well. Refrigerate until picnic time. Serve at room temperature.

Baked Beans

1 pound navy beans
1 quart hot water
1/2 pound lean sliced
    bacon, minced
1 large onion, minced
2 tablespoons prepared
    mustard

1 teaspoon salt
1 teaspoon black pepper
1/2 cup dark molasses
1/2 cup brown sugar
4 tablespoons maple
    syrup
1-1/2 cups water

Wash beans and put in large saucepan. Cover with 1 quart (4 cups) water. Bring to boil for 5 minutes. Turn off heat, cover pan and let set for 1 hour.

After 1 hour, turn heat back on low and simmer beans for 1 hour, or until beans are tender.

Meanwhile, in a large heavy pan, cook minced bacon until browned. Remove bacon and reserve. Pour off all but 4 tablespoons of fat. Reduce heat and sauté onion until tender. Stir in mustard, molasses, sugar, salt, pepper, syrup and 1-1/2 cups water. Add the drained beans, mixing well.

Transfer bean mixture to a large baking casserole, cover and bake in a preheated oven at 300 degrees for 1 hour. Reduce heat to 250 degrees, adding additional water as needed to keep beans from drying out. Bake 1 more hour, or until beans are tender and browned.

Chocolate-Cherry Brownies

1/2 cup butter
4 ounces unsweetened
　chocolate
2 cups sugar
4 eggs
1 teaspoon rum extract
2 teaspoons ground
　cinnamon

1/2 teaspoon salt
1-1/4 cups flour
1 cup chopped walnuts
1 7.5-ounce container
　glacé cherries

Melt butter and chocolate in saucepan. Let cool. In separate bowl, mix next 5 ingredients. Gradually add flour. Beat until smooth. Mix in chocolate. Add nuts and cherries. Spread mixture in 9 x 13-inch greased pan. Bake 35 minutes at 350 degrees. Cool before cutting 3-inch squares from pan. Makes approximately 12.

Cherry Sauce

1-1/2 cups cherry
　preserves

1/2 cup water
1 tablespoon sugar

Combine cherry preserves, water and sugar in a saucepan. Bring to a boil for 15 minutes until slightly thickened. Purée in a food processor and return to pan. Serve warm.

TO ASSEMBLE DESSERT:
Place a brownie square on a dish with a scoop of vanilla ice cream (if available). Top with warm cherry sauce.

Sangria

1 bottle dry red wine
1 ounce Brandy
Juice of 1 fresh orange
Juice of 1 lemon or lime
2 ounces sugar
6 very thin orange slices

6 very thin lemon slices
6 slices of any fresh fruit
   such as peaches, or
   15–20 fresh grapes.
1 bottle club soda
   (optional)

Mix wine, Brandy, fruit juices, and sugar until well blended. Chill. Just before serving, add club soda, if using, and fruit slices. Serve from a well chilled pitcher with lots of ice cubes.

About 4 servings

Sangria Champagne

1 ounce Triple Sec
1 ounce sugar, to taste
3 ounces grapefruit juice
Several dashes of lime
   juice

1 bottle of Brut
   Champagne, chilled
1 lime, sliced very thin

Mix all ingredients except Champagne, and chill. Pour into punchbowl or pitcher with lots of ice. Add Champagne, slowly, and stir gently.

About 4 servings

Postscript

If your book, gift or gourmet store does not have these books of ours, you may order them by telephone, fax, e-mail and mail. They are also available at our web site:
<Foodandwinecookbooks.com>

The Wine-Lovers Holidays Cookbook
Menus, Recipes & Wine Selections for Holidays
Entertaining $ 9.95 plus $3 S&H

Cooking with Wine
86 American Winery Chefs Share 172 of Their Favorite
Recipes for Cooking with Wine and Pairing Wine with Food
                                     $ 14.95 plus $3 S&H

The Wine Country Cookbook
128 of America's Finest Winery Chefs Share 204 of Their
Best Recipes with You $ 14.95 plus $3 S&H

The California Wine Country Herbs & Spices Cookbook, New & Revised Edition
A Collection of 212 of the Best Recipes by 96 Winery Chefs
and Winemakers, Featuring Herbs & Spices
                                     $ 14.95 plus $3 S&H

The Great Little Food With Wine Cookbook
76 Cooking with Wine Recipes, Pairing Food with Wine,
How and Where to Buy Wine, Ordering Wine in a
Restaurant $ 7.95 plus S&H

To order, call toll free (800) 852-4890, fax (707) 538-7371, e-mail HoffPress@world.att.net, or write to Hoffman Press, PO Box 2996, Santa Rosa, CA 94505-0996. We accept Mastercard, VISA, Discover and American Express credit cards.

Your money back if you're not delighted!